MORNING SICKNESS IS NOT "ALL IN YOUR HEAD"

For the thousands of pregnant women who suffer from morning sickness, this knowledgeable book offers welcome solutions to a very real and sometimes debilitating problem. By taking a nutritional approach to the relief of nausea, and other unpleasant symptoms associated with morning sickness, this survival guide helps you identify the foods and smells you should try to avoid, as well as the foods that provide relief. In addition to nutritional advice, you will find information about the causes of morning sickness; other women's stories; charts, tables and lists to enable you to monitor your situation; and other recommendations to get you through this temporary difficulty safely, naturally, and effectively.

NO MORE MORNING SICKNESS

MIRIAM ERICK, R.D., M.S., is a registered dietitian at The Brigham and Women's Hospital in Boston. Practicing as part of the in-patient obstetrical units, she is a specialist in diabetes and hyperemesis gravidarum (morning sickness) management. She is a member of the American Dietetic Association, the American Medical Writers Association, and the International Childbirth Education Association. She lives in Brookline, Massachusetts.

NO MORE MORNING SICKNESS

A Survival Guide
for Pregnant Women

MIRIAM ERICK, R.D., M.S.

A PLUME BOOK

PLUME
Published by the Penguin Group
Penguin Books USA Inc., 375 Hudson Street,
New York, New York 10014, U.S.A.
Penguin Books Ltd, 27 Wrights Lane,
London W8 5TZ, England
Penguin Books Australia Ltd, Ringwood,
Victoria, Australia
Penguin Books Canada Ltd, 10 Alcorn Avenue,
Toronto, Ontario, Canda M4V 3B2
Penguin Books (N.Z.) Ltd, 182-190 Wairau Road,
Auckland 10, New Zealand

Penguin Books Ltd, Registered Offices:
Harmondsworth, Middlesex, England

First published by Plume/Meridian, an imprint of New American
Library, a division of Penguin Books USA Inc.

First Printing, June, 1993
10 9 8 7 6 5 4 3 2 1

 REGISTERED TRADEMARK—MARCA REGISTRADA

Library of Congress Cataloging-in-Publication Data
Erick, Miriam.
    No more morning sickness : a survival guide for pregnant women /
Miriam Erick.
      p. cm.
    Includes bibliographical references.
    ISBN 0-452-26983-0
    1. Morning sickness—Prevention. I. Title.
RG579.E73 1993   92-43578
618.2′4—dc20   CIP

Printed in the United States of America
Set in New Baskerville
Designed by Leonard Telesca

A NOTE TO THE READER

The ideas, procedures, and suggestions contained in this book are not intended as a
substitute for consulting with your physician. All matters regarding your health require
medical supervision.

To all the women who chose to become mothers, especially
Susan, Lisa, Janet, Patricia, and Maryann

Contents

Acknowledgments

Thanks and appreciation are extended to the following persons for their support and guidance during the creation of this book:

To Frederick D. Frigoletto, M.D., Vice-chairman, Department of Obstetrics and Gynecology, Brigham and Women's Hospital, Boston; Jeff Ecker, M.D.; Marc Lauffer, M.D.; Enrique Africano, M.D.; B. Feinberg, M.D.; Susan Berman, M.D. To Dianne Pinegar; Richard Pinegar, M.D.; Michael Miller, M.D., Ph.D., medical director, Mercy Hospital, Portland, Maine; A. T. Champion; W.G. Rogerson; Priscilla Bolte, M.S.N., R.N.; Marcia Myers Marwell; and Nancy Beth Volk. To my colleagues on the Fuller/"High Risk" Obstetrics and Post-partum units at Brigham and Women's Hospital, especially Kathleen Costigan, R.N., M.P.H.; Judie Commeau, R.N.; Priscilla Peavey, R.N.; Rosemary Foy, R.N.; Holly Hughes; Christine Harker, R.N.; Arlene Buck, R.N.; Anne Korpi, M.S.W.; and Eileen Sheehan and Lynn Eccles, as well as many others.

To Carolyn Crimmins Hintlian, M.P.H., R.D., Massachusetts General Hospital; Sherri Hayes, Ph.D., R.P.T., Director, Division of Physical Therapy, University of Miami; Nadine Braunstein, M.S., R.D.; Nancy Clark, M.S., R.D.; Linda Hackfeld, R.D., M.P.H.; and Betsy Eykyn, M.S. To Jackie Kuhl at Paperchase, Katrina Pease, the reference librarians at Countway Medical Library at Harvard Medical School, the Coolidge Corner Branch of the Brookline Public Library, and Brown and Connolly Medical Bookstore. To Miles Richardson, Ph.D., Department of Anthropology, Louisiana State

University, and to Donald Vermeer, Ph.D., Department of Geography and Regional Sciences, George Washington University.

To current and former colleagues in the Department of Nutritional Services at Brigham and Women's Hospital, especially to Pat Gleason-Claydon, M.S., R.D.; Kathy McManus, M.S., R.D.; Mary Ellen Collins, M.Ed., R.D., Director; to Arlene Erceg Langseth, M.S., R.D.; Janet Washington, M.P.H., R.D.; Julie Webber, R.D.; Linda Weinberg, R.D.; Sigrid Schumann; and Maryann McDonough, R.D. To Rancy Bye, M.S., R.D.; and Maureen McBurney, M.S., R.D.; Director of Nutrition Support Services, Brigham and Women's Hospital.

To Howard Jacobson, Ph.D., School of Public Health of the University of South Florida; Carole Roberts; Kay George; Tanya Hayes; Judy Reid; Jackie Connolly; Antigone Letisou, R.D.; Sylvia Klein Olkin; Melodi Peters, R.D.; Susan Sherman, R.N.; Judy Gunderson; Maryann McGinn, M.D.; Judith Shabert, M.D., M.P.H., R.D. OB/GYN, Harvard Community Health Plan; Ellen Seely, M.D.; and Kathy Fairbanks, Ph.D., New York Medical College, Valhalla, New York, and the University of Bridgeport (Connecticut). To my nutrition assistants Grace Pierre, Ageet Virdi, Lola Wattree, Theresa Kelly, and Lenora Lewis. To all my clients, especially Jana, Carrie, Michelle, Kathleen, and Nancy. Lastly to my family, especially my sisters Sandy, Liz, Annette, and Terry, and to my marvelous niece and six super nephews.

My gratitude goes to Leza Hatch, M.A., R.P.T, for all her help, to Helen Haddad for the best editorial assistance a writer could ever hope to find, and to my agent Beth Backman, who dangled the carrot on a stick throughout. And I owe special thanks to Deb Brody, my editor at New American Library, for extraordinary insight in the field of women's health.

Foreword

Morning sickness is as old as human pregnancy, and nearly every pregnancy book mentions it somewhere. But the thousands of pregnant women who suffer through it each year know it's a more serious problem than a paragraph here or a few lines there can adequately address. Considering how common an ailment morning sickness is, the paucity of literature on it is astounding.

Some women are fortunate and have only mild or moderate discomfort for a few weeks. For others, however, morning sickness can be persistent and crippling, robbing them of the joys of expectant motherhood, with insomnia, extreme fatigue, and relentless nausea for most or even all of the duration of pregnancy. Women want answers to this problem that go beyond advising them to eat Saltine crackers. This book has them.

You can and should consult your obstetrician and/or a dietitian for treatment of morning sickness, because it may be that antinausea medication or an alteration of your diet will relieve you of your symptoms. It's important to know, however, that by no means does the medical community have *the* definitive solution to this problem, and that the power to reduce or alleviate symptoms may lie in your own hands.

Because each pregnancy is different, what triggers a bout of morning sickness varies from woman to woman—for some, it may be the way a person's breath smells, for others, it may be humid weather, or even something as seemingly benign as a glass of cold water. Miriam Erick wrote this book with this in mind and interviewed several women who devised their own strategies to counter morning sickness. With this book in hand, you too can learn to identify what triggers your morning sickness and can develop your own techniques and diet for relief.

Morning sickness is *not* in your imagination. You don't have to accept the opinions of those who think you're exaggerating your discomfort or the advice of those who say "Just grin and bear it." Miriam Erick has seen firsthand how devastating morning sickness can be, and her knowledge and insights are invaluable tools that will help you discover how best to manage your particular symptoms. Becoming a mother should be one of the most rewarding experiences of your life, and instead, it may be marred by the fear, anxiety, and anger caused as much by the inattention of medical literature to the problem as by morning sickness itself. *No More Morning Sickness* fills that gap.

You may only be able to eat rice cakes, tofu, and cream cheese; you may have to sleep with the window open in the dead of winter, or sit leaning to your left on a bus or train. That's all right. Miriam's book reminds you that it's your body and your pregnancy. Do whatever works for you.

Frederick D. Frigoletto, M.D.
Vice Chairman, Department of Obstetrics and Gynecology
Brigham and Women's Hospital
Boston, Massachusetts

NO MORE MORNING SICKNESS

Introduction

Whatever the degree of your symptoms, *No More Morning Sickness: A Survival Guide for Pregnant Women,* is designed to help you manage this common but often debilitating problem of pregnancy.

Statistics indicate that 50 to 90 percent of pregnant women suffer to some degree from morning sickness. Some women experience only mild nausea and vomiting for a few days or weeks; others struggle with severe nausea for all nine months. For centuries, the cause of morning sickness remained a mystery, prompting a variety of bizarre remedies, which you will read about in Chapter 9. In 1933, a doctor writing about this subject in the British medical journal *The Lancet* called morning sickness "a disease of theories." Today, substantial evidence indicates that the dynamics of hormones in pregnancy play a critical role in this universal syndrome.

This book is the first to be devoted exclusively to the care of women suffering from the common ailment of morning sickness. It's designed to help you, the pregnant woman, as well as your family, friends, and colleagues understand how diet can ease symptoms and help keep you healthy and happier.

How to Use This Book

No More Morning Sickness contains information about the possible causes of morning sickness, its history, people's reactions to it

—your own and those of others—and available resources. I've included dietary suggestions and recipes. You'll also find charts, tables, and lists to help you monitor your own situation. You may want to make copies of these.

If you're in the midst of a morning sickness crisis, you might go first to the practical chapters on food management, Chapters 4 and 5, or the chapter on dealing with hospitalization, Chapter 11. Then you can go back to the other chapters for a clear understanding of what morning sickness is all about.

CHAPTER 1

What Is Morning Sickness, Anyway?

Morning sickness seems to be a universal complaint with individual variations. It can combine some or all of the following symptoms, with different durations and levels of intensity: nausea, vomiting and retching; aversion to odors (some of which previously might have been considered pleasant), bright lights, loud noises, and snug-fitting clothes; sensitivity to invasion of personal space, perhaps better described as low-level claustrophobia.

The syndrome has been written about for at least four thousand years. The first mention of nausea and vomiting during early pregnancy was found in an Egyptian papyrus scroll dating to about 2000 B.C. Hippocrates described the same symptoms in about 400 B.C. These symptoms were later referred to as *maux de coeur,* which means "sickness of the heart." The French expression, *mauvais coucheur,* or in the case of the pregnant women, *mauvaise coucheuse,* seems to describe some of the subtle manifestations of morning sickness fairly well. This phrase means literally a bad bedfellow or someone who's hard to live with—which certainly describes any person who has the misfortune to feel waves of nausea the second she wakes up.

Smells, as I've mentioned, can have a lot to do with morning sickness, so much in fact that I've devoted Chapter 8 to this subject. Morning sickness is exacerbated if you sleep with the bedroom windows closed, making the air in the room quite stale by morning. The smaller the room, the staler the air. Bedroom air may be worse in the morning if the bedroom is too close to a kitchen, a bathroom, or the bedroom of an incontinent elderly person or young child.

Everybody knows that "morning breath" can be fierce, and what your bed partner ate the night before can also be a concern. A sleeping body gives off "fumes" all night, either by exhaling or in perspiration. Strong smelling foods and beverages such as onions, broccoli, sausages, and beer tend to make their presence known.

People of different regions also have different body odors as a group, again thanks to diet. The perspiration of Eskimos reflects the salted and smoked fish which is their staple; the perspiration of Japanese shows their high consumption of raw fish. To Eastern people, Americans have a "buttery" smell or smell like sheep. People working with certain minerals, notably selenium and tellurium, have been reported to give off a garlic-like odor. This information may be helpful in understanding why some women with morning sickness simply cannot sleep in the same room or bed with their mates without experiencing an increased level of nausea.

It's Not Just in the Morning

In spite of the name, morning sickness doesn't only happen in the morning. One researcher found that only 20 percent of women studied who experienced morning sickness had problems in the morning. This group of women had symptoms that persisted throughout the day.

If morning sickness is more of a problem for you in the morning, it may be because of a too-sharp transition from sleep to wakefulness. Abrupt motions, such as reaching to turn off a noisy alarm clock, can also disturb your equilibrium. As you start to move around at the beginning of the day, you may feel increased awareness of negative sensations. Even the movement of a restless bed partner can contribute to the morning sickness of pregnancy.

In a study of 244 women in the first trimester, half felt sick mainly in the morning. Less than 10 percent felt sickest either in the evening or in both the morning and the evening. Roughly one-third felt sick all day long and about one in eight had such severe nausea and vomiting that ordinary activity was impossible.

How Long Does It Last?

There's also a popular assumption that morning sickness goes away at the end of the first trimester, by week 13 of the pregnancy. This idea has been disproved by several well-controlled studies. One involved 414 pregnant women. The researcher found that 10.6 percent reported no symptoms, in contrast with 86.5 percent who experienced nausea; 53 percent experienced vomiting with nausea. Of the women who suffered from nausea in early pregnancy, about 25 percent were still having it at week 20. An unstated number continued to feel nausea until the end of the pregnancy. This study showed the average duration of morning sickness was 17.3 weeks, 4 weeks longer than most doctors and books cite.

When I interview pregnant and post-partum women, many say the nausea subsides at four or five months. However, I have also spoken with and cared for women whose nausea, with intermittent vomiting, continued to the day of delivery.

An Australian report speculated that 20 percent of all women with nausea and vomiting continue to suffer to the end of their pregnancies—not a pleasant prospect. However, being aware of these observations may be helpful when the first weeks come and go and the nausea and vomiting don't.

Women, their families, and their doctors often express frustration about trying to cope with the nausea and vomiting of morning sickness because of their often unpredictable waxing and waning. There may be a few great days between bouts, when all begin to think life is back to normal. Often, once a woman starts to feel better after a seemingly endless period of being sick, she tackles waiting projects with a vengeance. But morning sickness can recur without warning.

Relapse

A new cycle of nausea, vomiting, or both probably stems from a combination of factors: continuing changes in the amount of hormones produced during pregnancy, failure to consume enough fluids, and a major "trigger," usually a smell. To avoid a relapse, you need to avoid smells, noise, bright light, and major activities, such as commuting to work, household cleaning, family parties with copious amounts of aromatic foods. You must use trial and error to find foods that can break the nausea and vomiting cycle. (See Chapter 5, "Managing Morning Sickness with Food" for more details.) It's difficult not to get discouraged and angry during this time, but "the miserables" do go away eventually.

Theories, Ideas, and Hunches

As I've said, morning sickness is not always limited to early pregnancy, and it can be life-threatening. Although there are many theories about the causes of this problem, and no treatment which guarantees relief, any woman afflicted with morning sickness can do a great deal to manage her care.

You and your family, friends, and co-workers should understand that a pregnant woman suffering from nausea and vomiting (1) is not an isolated phenomenon, (2) is not basically neurotic or unhealthy, and (3) is not at any increased risk of having a damaged fetus.

The symptoms of morning sickness are listed in the table opposite. Many women experience only the "mild" symptoms, but morning sickness can progress from mild to severe. If it becomes so severe that hospitalization is necessary, it is called hyperemesis gravidarum.

Why some women get sicker in early pregnancy than others remains a mystery. Over the years many theories have been proposed, modified, and discarded. Ten current hypotheses are briefly presented below, which provide a basic understanding of the physiological changes that occur in a woman's body during pregnancy and may contribute to morning sickness.

Lowered Blood Sodium

Some researchers suggest that the discomforts of morning sickness may be associated with the biochemical changes that take place in the body of a newly pregnant woman, mainly the lowering of blood sodium. Increases in the levels of hormones start in early

Symptoms of Morning Sickness

Mild	Severe
Nausea with or without vomiting	Nausea and vomiting, not limited to a specific time
Worst in the morning on rising	Possible weight loss
Possible weight loss	Intolerance of cold
Intolerance of cold	Constipation
Possible constipation	Difficulty eating or drinking
Ability to eat between periods of nausea	Inability to perform activities of daily living
Ability to fall asleep	Difficulty falling asleep but relief with sleep
Appropriate urine output	Scant and highly concentrated urine output
Lying down helpful	Lying down more helpful in a dark, quiet room
Tiredness (avoiding fatigue extremely important in reducing nausea)	Extreme fatigue (may often wake from a nap because of nausea)
Provoked by heat or cold	Nausea aggravated by physical temperature
	Blood electrolyte levels concentrated, indicating dehydration
	Ketone positive (means stored fat is being burned as energy intake is below biological needs)
	Slow or impaired thinking
	Decreased attention span

Symptoms of Morning Sickness (Continued)

Mild	Severe
	Decreased motivation
	Decreased performance both mentally and physically
	Increased anxiety
	Boredom
	Symptoms aggravated by motion (either visual [i.e., TV close-ups and rapid scene changes] or physical [i.e., stop and go motion of a car or vehicle])
	Poor skin tone
	Dry, shrunken tongue
	Aching eyeballs, difficulty focusing with rapid visual changes

pregnancy and cause a number of changes, including an increase in the amount of water in the body which results in a higher volume of plasma. Plasma is the fluid portion of the blood; red blood cells form the solid red portion. This increase in the fluid proportion of the blood may lower the proportion of sodium, a major mineral. It's speculated that osmoreceptors (nerve endings that can detect alterations in blood compositions) adjust to this biochemical change over time, yet no one has figured out exactly when this might occur. However, low blood sodium can cause nausea, vomiting, and fatigue.

Baroreceptors, also known as stretch receptors, may also play a part in keeping sodium temporarily low. These receptors are found in the walls of the heart and blood vessels. Baroreceptors allow the blood vessels to relax or contract, depending on the influence of certain peptides and hormones. For example, if urine output is low, the baroreceptors might relax so more blood and fluid are directed to the kidneys. A stress response due to adrenaline might cause a constriction of these same blood vessels, and reduce blood flow. When blood pressure falls, whether because of vomiting or inadequate consumption of fluid, baroreceptors trigger a set of physiological responses to counteract the drop. A hormone called ADH (anti-diuretic hormone) also known as vasopressin, is secreted. It helps the body retain water, and less urine is excreted. However, unless salty foods or beverages are consumed, the amount of sodium in the body can stay low.

Adjustment of the Brain's Chemical Sensors

Another explanation focuses on the role that chemoreceptors in the brain may play. Chemoreceptors are nerve endings that can detect changes in the components of the blood, such as sodium, glucose, hormones, and oxygen. It's speculated that the dramatic rise in many hormones, especially estrogens, that comes with pregnancy precipitates nausea and vomiting in women who adjust more slowly to the increased levels.

Metabolism of Pregnancy Hormones

There is also a theory that the pregnancy hormones and their by-products put extra stress on the liver, the organ responsible for filtering the blood. Although the liver has a tremendous capacity for work, some researchers believe that it's the additional metabolic stress of pregnancy which causes changes in liver functions that in turn, result in nausea and possibly vomiting. This hypothesis is supported by research which shows that some women taking oral contraceptives have undergone small changes in their blood chemistries which originate from the liver. Birth-control pills contain various levels of estrogens and progesterone and some women taking the pills experience nausea and vomiting. Many women eventually adapt to the side effects; those who don't often stop using oral contraceptives.

Slower Emptying of the Stomach

Some prenatal nutrition experts report that pregnancy hormones slow down the emptying of the intestinal tract and stomach. It's thought that a more slowly working intestinal tract can cause nausea and may help explain morning sickness. Nausea in pregnancy has actually been shown by a test called an electrogastrogram to precede changes in muscular activity in the stomach.

Rising Hormone Levels

A woman produces more than thirty hormones during her pregnancy. The major hormones increase dramatically in the early weeks. From weeks 4 to 6, the increases in three major hormones amount to a doubling of the total level of hormones in the blood. From weeks 6 to 8, the increases in these three hormones add up to about 50 percent in the total levels of hormones in the blood. From weeks 8 to 10, the hormone levels double again. Weeks 10 to 12 bring a new major increase to a level which stays fairly constant until week 14. At 14 weeks a total of seven major hormones are present and the proportions of each have changed since the beginning of the pregnancy. Hormone levels begin to taper off at week 16, with the number of major hormones decreasing to five.

Interestingly, the total level of hormones rises again at week 20, when two new hormones appear. The total hormone level, although different, is about twice what it was four weeks earlier. These changes in hormone levels may be one cause of nausea and vomiting.

Left vs. Right Ovary

A Swedish research team found that women whose pregnancies originated from the right ovary were significantly more affected by nausea and vomiting than women whose pregnancies originated from the left ovary. It was speculated that the progesterone produced by the corpus luteum which surrounds the fertilized egg may be metabolized more rapidly when produced from the left ovary. Apparently the left ovarian vein drains into the left kidney vein, whereas the right ovarian vein drains into the inferior vena cava. The inferior vena cava is the major vein of the lower body which returns blood to the heart. Since kidneys are one of the organ systems responsible for clearing substances from the body, it's thought they may act to reduce the hormonal load produced during pregnancy.

Protection from Sexual Activity

Another theory proposes that nausea and vomiting had an evolutionary purpose, signaling the woman's mate that she was pregnant and causing disinterest in sexual activity. This disinterest could be a mechanism to protect the developing fetus from expulsion which could result from orgasmic contractions. Although this theory doesn't speculate what causes nausea and vomiting, it might provide stress relief for a woman that there might be a rationale for the suffering.

Fetal and Placenta Enzymes

Work in medical embryology suggests that powerful enzymes which help the fetus and placenta attach to the wall of the uterus may be responsible for the nausea and vomiting. As the placenta connects to the mother's biological system, it's possible that the resulting energy drain causes low blood sugar, hypoglycemia in the mother, which is often reported during pregnancy. Low blood sugar has been associated with nausea.

Protection from Toxins in Foods

A toxicologist from California speculates that the nausea and vomiting of pregnancy is nature's way of avoiding an accumulation of toxic substances that may originate from food, which may eventually harm the fetus. Plants and herbs contain natural chemicals which serve as herbicides. Dr. Profet feels that since food stays in the stomach longer due to the influence of pregnancy hormones, the ingested food may be being evaluated for safety. If too many potential toxins are present, signals may be sent from the stomach to the brain, which in turn causes vomiting. The changing ratio of estradiol to progesterone, she feels, may be the sensing mechanism.

Heightened Senses

One of the major complaints I have collected in my years of caring for hospitalized women with debilitating morning sickness stems from a heightening of the senses. Smells can become triggers setting off cycles of nausea and sometimes vomiting. (See Chapter 8, "Noses.") Other triggers are some flavors, abrupt motion, bright lights, and loud noises.

In-depth interviews with women suffering from morning sickness provide an amazing view of the way the escalation in the sense of smell that often accompanies pregnancy can undermine the well-being of a previously healthy woman.

I believe that this enhanced sense of smell is a natural adaptive universal phenomenon. It might have had its beginning as a survival mechanism. As pregnancy advances, a woman's increased bulk decreases her ability to flee from danger. A sharpened sense of smell can give advance warning of danger before a fire, ozone before a storm, or perhaps the scent of a predator on the wind.

Research indicates that one of the major pregnancy hormones, estrogen, is responsible for the increase in sensitivity to odors. It seems that the tremendous increase in estrogen itself may be proportional to this new smell threshold. Many women say that their sense of smell is greatly affected during pregnancy. Every scent is described as being heightened, more powerful, more provoking. Since most people agree that an overwhelming smell can precipitate nausea, the heightened sensitivity to smell has a clear connection to the nausea.

CHAPTER 2

If You're Miserable,
You're in Good Company

Every woman who's had morning sickness has probably heard, "Try tea, toast, Jell-O," or "Don't think about it and it'll go away." For many women this sort of advice isn't worth much.

If you're suffering from fairly severe morning sickness, you undoubtedly feel alone in your experience of constant debilitating nausea. But you shouldn't, because literally millions of women every year share your situation. As I mentioned earlier, 50 to 90 percent of all women have some degree of gastrointestinal discomfit in early pregnancy. Some women adjust to the morning nausea with time. However several studies point out that between 36 and 76 percent of all women feel sick all day long, especially in the first trimester.

A research nurse investigated the degree of nausea and vomiting of 133 department women in five different obstetrical practices in Boston. All the pregnancies were at week 20 or earlier. Less than 10 percent of the women had not been nauseated at all in the two days before their doctors' visits. Twenty-three percent had been nauseated from 3 to 6 hours, 15 percent from 7 to 15 hours, 10 percent from 13 to 18 hours, and 17 percent more than 18 hours.

The women were also asked to rate the severity of their nausea in the two days before their visits to the doctor. Slightly over one-third described their nausea as "mild," 56 percent called it "moderate," and about 7 percent considered the nausea "severe." They were asked to tell the number of times they had vomited. Slightly less than two-thirds said they had had no vomiting, 27 percent had vomited from one to three times, 8 percent had vomited from four to six times, and 3 percent had vomited more than six times. The study did not find any correlation of adverse outcome with the varying episodes of vomiting.

Does Morning Sickness Mean Something Is Wrong?

You and your family will want to know that morning sickness is not a sign that something is wrong with the pregnancy. In fact, statistics indicate that women who experience nausea, in particular, are more likely to have successful pregnancies than those that do not. Morning sickness has also been associated with fewer spontaneous abortions and early miscarriage.

In 1972 the National Institute of Neurological Diseases and Stroke investigated the effects of morning sickness, looking for adverse outcome, and finding nothing significant, cautiously concluded that there did not appear to be any greater risk of delivering a low-birth-weight baby nor any increased risk of deformity or congenital malformation because of nausea and vomiting.

Most women who are affected by nausea, vomiting, and weight loss worry about the well-being of their babies. A woman may think, "This baby is so small! Isn't he or she affected by my weight loss?"

A German research team seems to have come up with an explanation of why babies born to mothers with the most severe form of morning sickness—hyperemesis gravidarum—aren't noticeably smaller. For some reason yet undetermined, the researchers found that the blood flow to the uterus of a woman affected by hyperemesis gravidarum was at least twice that of a healthy pregnant woman. With twice the blood delivering nutrients and oxygen to the developing fetus, this seems to be a compensatory system which protects the fetus from the mother's inability to consume adequate nutrition.

If you are not getting supervised prenatal care you could be at risk for serious dehydration and electrolyte imbalance. Adverse outcome resulting from untreated vomiting in pregnancy may be more common in societies where medical care is not readily accessible and medical reporting rare. For instance, when I cared for a hospitalized woman with severe morning sickness, her boyfriend told me about a distant cousin who died in a remote village in Nigeria because of untreated vomiting several years earlier.

Refractory vomiting, or vomiting which does not subside with a full complement of standard medical attention, may be a sign of other significant medical problems which are beyond the scope of this book: diseases of the gallbladder, kidney and liver, pancreatitis, appendicitis, intestinal tract diseases, and thyroid dysfunctions, to name but a few.

You may be more afflicted with vomiting than with nausea. If you've had previous problems with motion sickness, gastric distress, migraine headaches, and difficulty using birth control pills, your nausea may be more intense.

Morning Sickness and Vision

Some women who wear contact lenses find that the lenses get uncomfortable during pregnancy. This may be caused by rising estrogen levels, which can cause fluid retention and so affect the shape of the cornea. In turn, eye discomfort and vision can act as a trigger for morning sickness.

Morning Sickness and Eating Disorders

Women who have had eating disorders may experience more stress in dealing with morning sickness. Vomiting from morning sickness may not be easily distinguished from the vomiting that accompanies the "binge-purge" syndrome known as bulimia. A case of self-induced vomiting by an ex-bulimic woman, who was also pregnant, has been noted in the medical literature under a syndrome called "bulimia nervosa." Unfortunately it is unclear whether the woman was also suffering from morning sickness and was merely trying to find relief.

My clinical experience tells me that pregnancy-influenced, self-induced vomiting is more common than many experts know. It's my opinion that self-induced vomiting is an attempt to get relief from overwhelming chronic nausea. But women with a history of bulimia have asked me whether the bulimic response ever occurs without the woman's putting her fingers down her throat. I don't know the answer to this question, but I would speculate that the length of time in remission of the behavior would be a factor; that is, if the bulimia was an active behavior in the few months before conception and done frequently, probably. However, if the bulimic episodes are over a year or two old, I'd venture a guess, no.

Some women with no prior history of purge-type eating disorders resort to self-induced vomiting to ease morning sickness. One pregnant woman who reported episodes of self-induced vomiting was suspected of having an underlying eating disorder, but I found a thoroughly exhausted woman merely trying to find relief from the never-ending nausea. She said she was unable to leave her home for fear that eventually she would vomit in front of others. Although few women admit this concern, it is understandable and common; and in my observation, this "bulimia of pregnancy" does not seem to be confined to any particular socioeconomic group.

In one week two hospitalized women with severe morning sickness reluctantly admitted self-induced vomiting to me. They believed few people would be sympathetic to their miseries, and both worried about being branded "weird." One woman was being harassed by her husband's family because he had told them she made herself vomit. She was not only angry with him but desperate for relief, since she had had a previous abortion because of similar illness. One study found 60 percent of 43 women seeking abortion had nausea with retching or vomiting.

When a recovering anorexic suffers from morning sickness, family pressure may reappear if her interest in food dwindles. Whether a high estrogen level itself is responsible for a depressed appetite similar to that reported in pre-menstrual women is not known, but it is speculated.

Separating symptoms of morning sickness from symptoms of eating disorders seems to be especially difficult for women who have "cured" themselves through self-help because they may lack the reinforcement of others noting a change in behavior and attitude. In addition, a woman's knowledge that her body is about to change radically is often a major concern, and some professionals feel that some women have great difficulty accepting this fact, especially the super-fit and athletic-minded.

Professional and high-powered career women seem to have more difficulty coping with the newly acquired disability of nausea and vomiting because they regard themselves as "super-women." With fifty-plus work weeks and three nights of aerobic workouts, the loss of control and the feeling of not being physically on top of the world as usual may be devastating.

Getting Help

If you're having morning sickness and you feel isolated, seek out a sympathetic counselor to help you maintain your emotional equilibrium. Finding someone who has also experienced morning sickness and is sympathetic may be a herculean task. A therapist with a waiting room full of clients may respond with revulsion if one of his or her patients suddenly retches or vomits.

A well-qualified counselor should be sympathetic to any situation, even if she or he has never shared the experience. The woman in need of additional emotional support has the option of shopping around if the initial contact proves unsatisfactory. No one should settle for the therapist recommended by the doctor's office if the match is wrong.

Becoming housebound because of the unpredictable nature of the problem is not unusual. Should this happen to you, telephone contact is vital. Since nausea and vomiting don't keep scheduled appointments of any sort, even telephone contact can become iffy. To solve that problem, you should make it known beforehand that you may need to hang up abruptly. Some women find talking a way to keep nausea down; others find just the opposite. One woman whose job required a lot of personnel training and speaking before groups said that after she'd talked for a long while, it felt as though someone was pressing a finger into the back of her throat, and she suffered retching. We figured out that what was probably happening was that her gag reflex was more sensitized with prolonged tongue motion which occurs with talking. (See the tongue diagram on page 181.) These places on the tongue are connected by the vagus (or wandering) nerve to various parts of the brain and body, notably the stomach. With increased pressure on these points, nausea can increase.

Every woman has her "good window," or the time of the day when she feels somewhat improved. Sometimes talking just a few seconds after this improved time has passed is enough to escalate nausea and generate more saliva. Saliva, as I'll explain more fully later on, can trigger nausea. Sometimes merely talking about food becomes another trigger.

One you understand what may trigger nausea or vomiting, it's helpful to share your discoveries with others.

CHAPTER 3

A Candid Look at Feelings

People who know you have morning sickness often ask how you're feeling. Some genuinely want to know; others come across as armchair quarterbacks. Expect a few to say something crude, stupid, or insensitive. You don't need to answer truthfully or answer at all if it's likely to prolong a conversation you'd prefer not to have. A quick comment or a smile may be all you can muster while struggling to maintain equilibrium. It may help to be prepared for certain comments.

Some people ask the standard questions but don't really want an honest answer. A typical comment: "But you look pretty good." Of course, when quiet nausea turns into a case of dry heaves or vomiting, fewer people want to continue the conversation or hang around and try to help.

Some people like to compare miseries. "Let me tell you how sick my sister Mary was. But she'd get up and drive fifty miles one way to work anyway!"

Some people seem to want to "rub it in" out of jealousy. From friends or relatives who've been trying for years to become pregnant, you might hear: "But you should be so happy you're pregnant."

Some people simply want to keep up on the local gossip. "So, June, you've lost *so* much weight, what do you weigh now? Isn't that bad for the baby? What is your doctor doing about it?"

Some people seem to try to make you feel guilty. "I don't know anybody else who can't or refuses to eat! Just eat! After all, this is going to be a grandchild of mine, and this business has to stop!" It might help to understand that this type of comment really says, "I'm worried about you and I've never seen you sick. I don't know what to do."

Many people feel compelled to respond when someone asks, "How are you?" The real answer may be, "Miserable." But most women figure the questioner probably wants to hear the brave but bland "I'm really fine." Women are somehow expected to bear up admirably, since "after all, it's *only* pregnancy!" Many women also want to avoid sounding wimpy and don't care to relive every private agony.

If you're a miserable mother-to-be the waxing and waning emotions you experience can range through the following (and beyond):

Anger—that you're so sick, and that others may expect standard, everyday "well-person" performance. Or anger with yourself because of your own disappointed expectations.

Guilt—because you resent the disruption of your life by morning sickness. Or guilt because the pregnancy was unplanned and you must decide whether to continue it.

Uncertainty—about how long your job, other commitments, and your whole life will stay on hold because of morning sickness, which makes getting through a day a full-time job in itself. Uncertainty about continuing the pregnancy because everyone is asking, "How come you're so sick?" or because of financial worries.

Weirdness and isolation—because none of the several dozen books about pregnancy you've flipped through discussed morning sickness in detail. You begin to think, "I must be the only person who ever feels like this! What's wrong with me?" Everyone you meet seems to say in total amazement, "Gee, I never met anyone before who has what you have!"

Exhaustion—You never feel or look rested even though you seem to sleep all the time. The bags under your eyes are sagging toward your knees. Your disposition may deteriorate.

Depression and ambivalence—Plans to go anywhere with anyone are on permanent hold because you never know whether it'll be a good day or a bad day. By now friends may not be calling so often.

Fear—You're afraid "it" (the nausea and vomiting) will never end. Particularly if you've never been this sick before, it can be tough to believe that this isn't something more than morning sickness. You're not convinced your doctor is totally competent—if he or she was, wouldn't you be better by now?

Abandonment—Who stays around when your nausea and vomiting are at their worst? Perhaps the only person who'll really understand is your mother, maybe because mothers have gone through a lot of mess and unpleasantness in their time. But if there are bumps in your relationship with your mother, smoothing them out in the middle of your physical crisis may be a tough job.

Betrayal—Maybe your spouse or significant other says, "It's all in your head," or, "This could stop if you really tried," then announces that he can't be much help anyway and goes about his usual activities. Since your situation is partly his doing, you're upset that he isn't around when you need him.

Unattractiveness—The best you can seem to do now is open your eyes in the morning. Makeup may be totally out of the picture. You've heard you're supposed to glow, but it's tough to be radiant in baggy sweats with filmy teeth and oily skin. Nobody ever mentioned this might be part of the deal.

Vulnerability—Some men who have seen family members, especially their mothers, become terminally ill find it difficult to cope with a woman suffering from nausea and vomiting. Seeing you bedridden can generate an overwhelming foreboding and sense of vulnerability, which saps energy and is difficult to surmount alone.

Of course, there is a way you can "share" the sensation of queasiness with the unsympathetic. Buy a few tickets to an Omni Max theater performance and suggest that your husband take a friend, "just to get out of the house and enjoy yourself"—or present the tickets to your doctor or a coworker or whoever you think needs the experience. In an Omni Max theater the wide screen is bowed out toward the audience. Although the cinematography is spectacular, the rapid zoom techniques make a good percentage of the audience moderately nauseated. This experience may demonstrate just how debilitating low-level nausea can be.

A great way to purge nasty negative emotions is by using "food voodoo." This little game may sound juvenile to some people, but it works well to dissipate anger. You can use any sort of food, but crunchy ones work best. Take a few carrot sticks or celery stalks and pretend they're the legs or arms of the person you're angry with. Bite down hard and work for the loudest noise possible. With every crunch, say to yourself, "There, I got even and now I feel better!" Roundish raw vegetables such as radishes, florets of cauliflower, and mushrooms make nice food voodoo heads. Gingerbread men are a good choice as well, for obvious reasons.

Getting rid of stress this way can help relax the muscles in your gastrointestinal tract, making for better digestion. When you play food voodoo, you tend to eat foods with high fiber and high water content, which helps prevent constipation. There's some evidence that chemical compounds in ginger work to stimulate the appetite and calm the gastrointestinal tract, so munching gingerbread men may bring a double benefit.

You may not experience all of these emotions, but just knowing that others have trod the same path should give some comfort, a sense of sisterhood, and optimism. Emotions often grow more powerful when you keep them to yourself; sharing your troubles can divide your worry and lower stress. Do your best to find someone you can talk with regularly.

CHAPTER 4

The Role of Nutrition

If you're going through morning sickness, it's critical that you maintain the best nutrition you can manage. You need to take in calories every day to make the energy you need to function.

This chapter explains the roles of carbohydrates, proteins, calories, and ketones, as well as the dangers of dehydration. (See Chapter 12 for more information on the various food groups.) The more you understand about the way these elements function, the easier it will be for you to make sound decisions about nutrition while you're enduring morning sickness.

Carbohydrates

Carbohydrates—grains, cereals, fruits, and vegetables—provide various forms of energy, both quick and sustained. Quick energy comes from simple carbohydrates, or sugars (in cookies and candy, for example), which are rapidly digested. More sustained energy comes from the more complex carbohydrates, the starches, which are more slowly digested. The body can store only a small amount of carbohydrate. Quite a small portion is stored in the liver, in the form of glycogen. Muscles also store a small amount of glycogen, which is rapidly used up with activity. However, if more carbohydrate calories are taken in than are needed, the body will store this extra energy as fat. During times of limited intake, fat breakdown will provide calories or energy for the body to burn.

Protein

Meat, fish, cheese, eggs, legumes, and tofu are protein foods. A certain amount of the protein foods you consume are used to keep muscles intact. During pregnancy, protein supports the growth of the new fetus as well as supplying the needs of the mother. Many of the body's enzymes and hormones are made of amino acids, which come from the breakdown of protein. When more protein is eaten than needed, the surplus is stored as fat. Any extra fat eaten (butter on toast, mayonnaise in a tuna fish sandwich, etc.) over your daily caloric needs also gets stored in the fat bank.

Of the three components of food—carbohydrates, protein, and fat—protein requires the most water to process, because the body must rid itself of excess nitrogen, an element found almost exclusively in proteins. Nitrogen is eliminated from the body mainly in the urine. Many protein foods have a relatively low water content (see Chapter 9, "Special Concerns"). If you eat a high-protein diet make sure you have an adequate fluid intake.

Calories and Ketones

Problems begin when a pregnant woman is unable to ingest the daily calories she requires. First her body uses up glycogen, a stored form of carbohydrate. Then it begins to use stored fat for energy, and then muscle. This is what normally happens when you go on a weight-loss diet. One difference is that on a moderate weight-loss diet, the planned calorie deficit each day is probably only a few hundred calories. But severe nausea and vomiting are not planned, and the resulting calorie deficit is often beyond your control.

Assume for a moment that the average pregnant woman in her first trimester needs to consume 1,700 to 2,200 calories a day depending on height and prepregnancy body size and general activity. (Of note, the most recent Recommended Dietary Allowances, RDA's, don't add 300 calories per day for pregnancy until the beginning of the second trimester. This assumes, of course, that there are no unusual situations, such as weight loss caused by morning sickness.) When a pregnant woman is unable to take in (and keep down) the required maintenance calories, her body has no choice but to burn fat first and then burn muscle to make energy.

One of the by-products of burning fat, or fat metabolism, is the production of ketones. Ketones are keto-acids which give your breath a peculiar, fruity smell; they can be one of the factors responsible for the bad taste in the mouth that many pregnant women have. The body tries to get rid of ketones by exhaling them or passing them out through the urine. Producing large quantities of ketones can ultimately affect how much oxygen the blood can carry. Doctors usually check for urine ketones and take action before critical levels accumulate in the blood. The presence of large amounts of ketones indicates some degree of malnutrition. If the body is also becoming dehydrated, the ketone concentration in the blood can be even higher. Another reported effect from high levels of ketones is nausea. Ketones can be eliminated fairly quickly by eating small amounts of carbohydrates regularly.

The Dangers of Dehydration

Water is the nutrient most critical to life. When your fluid consumption doesn't satisfy your body's needs because nausea prevents you from eating and drinking, or because you keep vomiting, dehydration is often the consequence. Since dehydration has an immediate effect on all body functions, it calls for medical intervention—possibly a trip to an emergency room for outpatient fluid therapy.

Dehydration is a serious problem because it can affect your blood pressure. If your blood pressure gets too low, it can cause fainting, low urine output, and reduced nutrient supplies for the fetus—all potentially harmful. If you're suffering from these symptoms, a hospital stay may be necessary (see Chapter 11).

If vomiting becomes more severe, vital minerals (called electrolytes) are lost, along with gastrointestinal fluids. The major electrolytes are potassium, sodium, and chloride. Each plays an important role in body functions. Minerals help muscles to contract, especially the muscles of the heart, which pumps blood to all parts of the body. Lowered levels of potassium and sodium can result in weaker heart contractions or irregular heartbeats. When body fluid is lost, the volume of blood which the heart has to pump is also reduced.

Hospitalization

On occasion a hospital stay to correct dehydration is necessary. If this happens, morning sickness becomes known as hyperemesis gravidarum, which literally means abnormal *(hyper)* vomiting *(emesis)* by a pregnant woman *(gravid)*. Approximately 55,000 American women are hospitalized each year because of dehydration as a result of morning sickness.

One goal of this book is to help women avoid hospitalization. This can be done by identifying a number of situations which can precipitate and aggravate nausea into unrelenting vomiting and possibly dehydration.

How do you know if your morning sickness situation is going from bad to worse? The list of mild and severe symptoms in Chapter 2 contains some rules of thumb to measure progress.

A net weight loss does not always accompany morning sickness. Although many women who aren't able to eat regularly lose a few real and fluid pounds, not all do, for the following reasons:

1. The pregnancy hormones, especially estrogen, help the body retain fluid. Since body fluid is part of body mass, any gain or loss can make a difference when you get onto the scale. The pregnancy hormones also slow down the rate at which food goes through the body, and more calories are thought to be absorbed.

2. If weight declines slowly, the body sometimes readjusts its basal metabolic rate, becoming more efficient and using fewer calories—perhaps by lowering the body temperature a fraction, or by reducing the number of respirations or heartbeats in a given period. In addition, when you feel ill, you automatically reduce your physical activity, which again saves calories. Just as a point of reference, the number of calories needed to maintain the weight of a healthy adult is about 1 to 1.25 per minute, barring exercise

or extraordinary activity. This is the basal metabolic rate or the number of calories it takes to operate the body at rest. This works out to be about 1,440 calories for the average woman, 5 feet 5 inches tall and 120 pounds.

Dietitians add another 25 percent for usual activities, which in this example would work out to 360 calories, making the maintenance total about 1,800 calories a day.

Putting calories into perspective, a slice of toast, about 70 calories, will provide the average woman with enough fuel to operate metabolically for about one hour. For the father of the baby, an average, physically fit man weighing approximately 180 pounds, this same slice of toast will probably be used up in less than forty minutes. The reason for the difference is that most men have more muscle and less fat mass than most women; muscles use more energy than does fat mass.

3. You may eat more during your "good periods" than you realize. A switch from three cans of diet soda a day to five cans of regular soda means 800 calories, where, with diet soda the caloric contribution would have been zero, or perhaps 40 percent of a day's caloric requirement. Fifteen soda crackers could mean about 280 calories, or almost one-seventh of the average daily requirement of 2,000 calories.

Your perception that you're "starving" may be amplified because your food choices are often narrowed. The food suggestions generally given to sick women usually stick to the bland and white or tan foods. These suggestions come from families as well as health-care providers, having been handed down through the years as remedies that work for everyone.

4. Fluid losses with vomiting make weight loss difficult to assess from day to day. The time of day, the scale used, and the absence or presence of bowel movements can also change the weight picture.

Since everyone is concerned with weight changes, the smallest downward trend can spark panic, which may be a bit premature. A weight monitoring chart is provided on page 183 to help you plot the changes during your pregnancy.

Despite the apparent contradiction, many women achieve very high weight peaks in their pregnancies *because* of nausea and vomiting. Many find that eating something—anything—all the time makes them feel better, or at least "less horrible."

"Eating something specific" was the most reported strategy to ease nausea uncovered by a research study in 1989. Successful types of food were, in descending order, crackers, bread, fruit, cereal, dairy products, sweets, meats, and salty foods.

Digestion, for all intents and purposes, begins in the brain. Thinking about food—even dreaming—starts the digestive juices flowing. The process of chewing breaks down food mechanically at the same time that the enzymes in saliva begin to break down food chemically. The amount of saliva produced varies with the degree of saltiness or tartness, and the texture (smooth or rough) of a specific food. From the stomach, food moves through the gastrointestinal tract, again at varying rates. It is reported that high-fat meals stay in the stomach longer than do starchy low-fat meals, and that liquids empty out faster than do solid meals and saltier foods.

Bile, produced by the gallbladder, is released when fat is part of the diet. Some women with severe morning sickness develop "thick bile" or "sludge" if their intake of fluids drops abnormally low for long periods; this can contribute to gallbladder disease in pregnancy, since highly concentrated sludge can crystallize into small stones. Sometimes very small amounts of potato chips might help to empty the gallbladder periodically and prevent gallstones from forming. I worked with a woman who, pregnant with twins, was hospitalized with "sludge," a large weight loss, and continued nausea and vomiting. Her surgeons considered removing her gallbladder at the time of admission to avoid trickier surgery later in her pregnancy. Once we reduced her nausea, she was able to increase her consumption of fluid and food using watermelon. At home, she succumbed to an urge to eat a piece of fatty London broil, noting some immediate discomfort, followed by marked improvement, that continued to delivery. Afterwards she felt poorly periodically. A follow-up exam showed abnormal liver studies, possibly the result of early pregnancy exposure to job related toxic chemicals. This woman keeps me posted on her situation.

Food choices are often subconscious, and I believe we intuitively gravitate to the foods and beverages that make us feel comforted. It's important to note that the comfort food of a sick person will probably not be the comfort food of a well person. The care provider sees the woman with morning sickness in a dehydrated or semidehydrated state and naturally wants to encourage the woman to drink more liquids. The woman herself, however, is more inclined to eat solid foods, as they reduce her queasiness (however craves liquids to reduce the terrible sensation of thirst). The key to breaking the cycle of nausea and vomiting is to alternate food and liquid in the pattern which brings most comfort to the pregnant woman.

C H A P T E R 5

Managing Morning Sickness with Food

Without knowing it, most people are pretty ethnocentric and ego-centric about the foods they choose to eat. Getting people to deviate from their usual daily diets is difficult. Further, food is often categorized as good or bad; healthful or junk; tasty or "yukky"; recommended or *verboten;* or familiar (safe) or strange (suspect).

Food gets particular attention when someone is sick or pregnant. If you're sick *and* pregnant, you may find that everyone who has ever read anything about morning sickness becomes an instant expert. You'll undoubtedly be offered dozens of food solutions, mainly "Eat crackers," the traditional safe recommendation. For some women, this works. For others, a cracker is a long way from providing relief.

Books and articles that mention morning sickness—in most cases very briefly—cite similar remedies and routines of tea, dry toast, Jell-O, ginger ale, and soup. But following their advice doesn't necessarily mean your morning sickness will abate.

Figuring Out What to Eat

Ask yourself this question: What food or beverage would ease your nausea? Something salty, sour, bitter, tart, sweet, crunchy/ lumpy, soft/smooth, mushy, hard, fruity, wet, dry, bland, spicy, aromatic, earthy, hot, cold, thin, or thick? Generally speaking, these adjectives cover almost all foods and beverages. Interestingly, when you start to think about these characteristics, new lists of foods and beverages emerge. Each, of course, contains varying amounts of nutrients, water, and fiber. Each food or beverage may be successful under certain conditions only—for example, in the absence of other food aromas or at a particular time of day. Only by beginning a systematic search will you unearth possible answers. Keeping a daily food diary can be extremely helpful in discovering your tendencies. Your nutritionist can use such a diary to evaluate your diet and help you manage your weight.

Keeping foods in mind, consider the following questions: Would something salty reduce or aggravate the queasy feelings at this very minute? If yes, what food or drink comes to mind at this very moment? If it could be procured instantly, would you eat it? Why or why not?

Would something crunchy diminish your nausea? If yes, what sort of color or flavor would it have? What sort of food or beverage, however bizarre or atypical of your usual choices, appeals to you at this very moment? (Whether or not it's in season is immaterial. Most foods are available almost year-round at premium prices in specialty stores. It could be well worth a special trip and the extra money.) Keep asking these three or four questions until you've gone through all the food characteristic adjectives. You'll be surprised at the number of new foods and beverages that come to mind.

It's not uncommon for a woman first to find something she wants to eat in the salty, sour, bitter, or sweet category. It seems that if you can drive the sensation of thirst away with a food from one of these categories, drinking fluids follows more naturally. Recently, I had remarkable success when I gave one of my hospitalized morning sickness clients several Tootsie Rolls, which were what she requested and could eat and keep down. Several hours later she began drinking adequate fluids, and we broke her cycle of nausea and vomiting.

Another woman, admitted at least five times in her first trimester of pregnancy, found on her fourth admission that sour-cream-and-onion-flavored potato chips were the food that helped her break the cycle. Yet another, having been transferred to us after one month on intravenous feeding at another hospital, was eating within three days. Among the few changes that accompanied her transfer was an "ad lib" diet order—we served what she asked for. Whether it was her newly acquired habit of beginning her meals by dipping raw carrots and celery sticks into a cup of vinegar, or the discontinuation of her intravenous feedings, or a change in her medication routine that effected the improvement is difficult to know. Both the patient and her family found it odd that her new ritual of dipping the vegetables in vinegar seemed to help her eat more. After eating about three or four sticks each of raw celery and carrot, she would eat approximately three-quarters of each meal, and she drank at least 1½ quarts of fluid each day.

I've had much success with lemonade, probably because the high sugar and calorie content is masked by its tart/bitterness. From a nutritional management standpoint, the consequences of eating unconventional foods like those described in the three cases above are minuscule and often short-lived. I've found that the woman who chooses a novel food and can eat it almost at the moment she decides she wants to, has a greater likelihood of keeping nausea and vomiting at bay. One reason that women may not acknowledge the urge for novel foods is that more often than not they fall into the junk food category.

I've asked many women why they don't eat a junk food when it appeals to them, and the overwhelming answer is guilt. Prenatal guides that cover nutrition tout the benefits of good dietary habits, and rightly so. Many women believe that if they consume anything on the "do not eat" list, the baby will immediately suffer. While it's true that a pregnancy will benefit by better eating habits, eating well but vomiting, and taking antivomiting medication, are perhaps more harmful overall to both mother and baby.

Time Charts

Another question to ask and answer: What time of day is most associated with nausea or vomiting? Is the time of day the only factor, or is there a contribution (physical or emotional) from someone else? Rating the degree of nausea from 1 to 10, along with foods or beverages requested, at various times has been helpful for several women. (A chart is provided for data collection at the end of the book.) Recording these data may present you with a clearer picture of how to approach each day.

Stimuli: Good, Bad, or In-Between

Are there smells which seem more acute than before your pregnancy and add to your nausea? Are the smells temporary or permanent? Do you feel queasy because you've just awakened? Was the wake-up slow and gentle or startling? Are the lights too bright? Is there noise? If so, is it loud and irksome? What noise in particular is most irritating? Can it be reduced? Does it originate in your household or is it beyond your immediate control? If you're not vomiting and look fairly well, are you expected to perform either housework or office work? Do you feel pressure? From whom? Is your gastric distress the result of taking a prenatal vitamin, iron supplement, or medication? Or is it because you didn't take a medication on schedule?

Next ask: When you feel the absolute worst, if any food or drink could be delivered instantaneously, what would it be? Would the likelihood that you'd consume it be higher than average if you could have presto delivery? Does the urge to eat or drink evaporate while you're waiting for the food or beverage? How many minutes after you make a food request does your desire to eat diminish? What factors besides time are associated with the closing of the window of opportunity—noise, motion, a smell?

If you had to prepare the food yourself, did you lose your desire to eat because the sight of the food during preparation was overwhelming? Did any single ingredient cause this reaction, either by sight or smell? Or was standing in a kitchen with residual smells part of the problem? Will a solid food really do? Would a drink be preferable? How does a thick liquid feel compared to a thin liquid? What taste and texture craving is the strongest when your sickness is at its peak? What taste and texture cravings emerge when you're feeling better?

In what room of your house or apartment do you most enjoy eating? Which room is the worst? Is there any correlation between the time of day and the place where you eat? There are several areas to explore in attempting to find a pattern in the bad times. Many small, "invisible" factors can help you feel better or, as most women prefer to say, "less worse." These factors all seem to revolve around the senses: smell, taste, motion, sight, hearing, touch, and stress. I've added motion and stress to the original quintet of senses because they seem to be highly significant factors in successful management of morning sickness. Because they're difficult to measure, it's often hard for others to appreciate their intricate interrelationship, which contributes to your morning sickness. Consideration of these aspects can make the difference in your sense of well-being.

My interviews with hundreds of pregnant women, from every socioeconomic level and cultural corner, indicate that although the problem of morning sickness is universal, the solutions are highly individual. (See the vignettes presented in Chapter 13, "Real Stories from Real Women.")

Cravings

Back in 1957 two British researchers summarized information obtained from the BBC talk show *Is There a Doctor in the House?* on the topic of pregnancy. Women were asked to write in about their cravings. The reports from 820 pregnancies described 991 cravings, including 746 specific comments about food.

The most-craved foods were fruits (apples, oranges, lemons), followed by pickled food or raw cereal, then spices and condiments, and finally vegetables, especially tomatoes. About three-quarters of the women had two or more cravings simultaneously. One-quarter found coffee and tea distasteful. The researchers were taken aback by the number of women who stressed the seriousness of their cravings and the lengths to which they went to satisfy them. The survey also noted that a small percentage of women craved non-food items, such as coal, soap, laundry starch, clay, certain types of mud, disinfectant, and toothpaste. Apparently the toothpaste used in Great Britain in the late 1950s was a powdered variety of which a main ingredient was baking soda (mainly sodium bicarbonate), an effective antacid.

Two-thirds of the pregnant women in another British study said they craved fruit because the juiciness satisfied their thirst. That study also found frequent cravings for strongly flavored foods such as pickles, black (blood) pudding, licorice, potato crisps (chips), cheese, and kippers (smoked fish). Many women in the study said they found the sight of eggs revolting. Cravings for chocolates and other sweets were mentioned occasionally.

The craving for non-food items is called pica. Although pica has been reported many times in the medical literature, the actual number of cases seems to be quite small. Pica can be extremely harmful to both the mother and the fetus, especially if the mother eats something as bizarre as inner tubes or air fresheners (which have each been reported only once).

If you have any unusual cravings, discuss them with a doctor or nutritionist, who can assess whether they're associated with any short-term or long-term nutritional or other problems. These strange urges may simply be an attempt to reduce debilitating nausea. A doctor may suggest a change in medication as well as prenatal vitamin supplements. A registered dietitian or nutritionist can provide additional food suggestions and perhaps recipes.

The range of foods eaten by women around the world during early pregnancy is highly variable. See Chapter 7, "Other Times and Other Places," for further information.

Your Road to Self-Improvement

Recording successful food choices and other variables is extremely helpful. Use the charts provided on page 110. You can make as many copies of these charts as you need. The food lists which begin on page 40 are a good place to start. Make a check next to foods you've had success with. Cross out "No, never" foods and give "maybe" foods a question mark. It's important to evaluate familiar "comfort" foods. (Southern women often prefer bananas and mayonnaise on white bread, while several New England women told me their comfort food was cold seafood and spicy cocktail sauce.) If your family's favorite "comfort food" has become repulsive to you, you need to let the rest of the family know—especially if your mother or another relative is coming to help out for a few days.

More Problem Solving

Suppose you note that the worst time of the day is the morning. You can't even think about food or drink until 11 A.M. or your nausea rapidly escalates. But by 11 A.M., after adjusting to an upright position, making slow movements, and maintaining a quiet environment, you ask yourself what might ease your nausea, and "salty, dry, and crunchy" are the words that come to mind. How about potato chips? Do they appeal more than crackers? If so, there's no reason not to eat them. Other salty, dry foods might be cheese curls, popcorn, or pretzels.

Maybe ice cream works for you and sherbet doesn't. This is not the time to worry about the fat content. During a morning sickness crisis, any type of calorie you can keep down is a successful calorie. In the field of clinical nutrition, we call this sick-day meal management.

Say the adjectives that come to mind are "wet/dry, crunchy, cold." Consider watermelon or a frozen fruit pop. If you think "tart, cold, and thick" may do the trick, try Italian lemon ice, a lemonade mousse, or lemonade thickened with a modified cornstarch supplement called "Thick-It" or "Thick 'n Easy" (available in most pharmacies; see "References and Resources" at the back of the book).

Keep in mind that figuring out what you'll want to eat or drink two hours from now is like catching Jell-O in a fishnet—almost impossible. The invisible factors that control your condition (smells, hormones, blood chemistry, motion, fatigue, etc.) change constantly. I've worked with women whose taste buds screamed for salty foods when they felt sickest. As they improved, they craved foods that were "sweet and earthy."

One woman reported that she couldn't get out of bed until she ate a pile of very salty crackers. At midmorning she drank lemonade and iced tea loaded with lemon. At noon she wanted oranges; in midafternoon it was orange Creamsicles. If she didn't take an afternoon nap, nothing worked in the evening because her fatigue set off a bout of vomiting. After the nap, she got through the evening eating chocolates. This woman, a nutrition-conscious college graduate, taught health, physical education, and aerobics.

She had struggled to resist her urges to eat and drink lemonade, Creamsicles, and chocolates because she had always considered them "unnutritional." Eating according to the guidelines her doctor's office gave her at her second prenatal visit had met with zero success. When she finally gave in to her cravings, she was able to function enough to care for her two-year-old daughter and five-year-old son. As the weeks went on, she was slowly able to add one or two of the "recommended" foods without precipitating an episode of vomiting.

Keep in mind that each food contains as many as fifty known nutrients. Add those factors to the widely varying textures and tastes of foods and it's almost impossible to figure out why certain items work and others don't. But if you make a determined effort to record some of the general characteristics of the foods and beverages that work for you, you'll begin to see a pattern. It's all right to eat one food or one standard meal if that's the only thing you can keep down. (I call this "mono-eating.") Whatever works, use it.

Eating and Sleeping

When you go to bed, try to keep a window open at least one to two inches—unless, of course, noise is a problem or security is an issue. You might consider a small fan to provide soothing white noise. A well-ventilated room should decrease stale bedroom air in the morning. (One of the hospitalized women I cared for found the odor from a new vinyl mattress so offensive she had her husband bring in swimmer's nose clips.) If you've been vomiting in the middle of the night, wait at least an hour or two after your last meal before going to sleep. Otherwise, eating until you fall asleep will reduce the likelihood of low blood sugar on waking, which some sources claim causes nausea. Again, the watchword is do what feels best.

If you're exhausted and want to sleep immediately after eating, try lying on your right side. This may help empty your stomach faster, since the stomach empties from left to right. If you lie on your left side, your stomach must pump food "uphill," since the beginning of the small intestine, the duodenum, is connected to the right side of the stomach. Lying on the left side also seems to pool the stomach contents directly below the end of the esophagus. Since the tone of the esophageal sphincter muscle is thought to be relaxed by the presence of pregnancy hormones, it may be less effective in keeping the contents of the stomach contained.

Some books say not to eat right before going to bed, since sleep may be disturbed. Eating or drinking some foods or beverages does cause a problem for some women. The most common culprit is caffeine, found in coffee, tea, colas, and chocolate. But another substance, phenylethylamine, is also found in these items, as well as in aged cheeses, sausages, and pickled herring. Phenylethylamine can constrict small blood vessels, which can aggravate headaches and disturb rest.

Monosodium glutamate (MSG) is also reported to increase brain activity and heart rate in some people, which can disturb sleep. Commonly found in Chinese restaurant food, MSG also turns up in Mexican, French, American, and Italian dishes, as well as in many prepared grocery-store foods. The tastier the food, the likelier it contains MSG. Sauerkraut, meat tenderizers, and bouillon cubes contain lots of MSG. Sometimes it's disguised on the label as "natural flavorings" or HVP, hydrolyzed vegetable protein. My own experience is that MSG in a spicy evening meal will cost me more hours of sleep than several cups of coffee.

If you have success with certain foods and the nutrients they contain (rather than their tastes or textures) seem to be the connecting factor, stay with that approach. If you need more individual nutrient analysis, be sure to contact a registered dietitian (R.D.) who has a computer nutrient analysis program. (See "Selected References" at the back of the book.)

Foods to Try

The next few pages list the major food taste and texture categories. Keep in mind that you could probably add hundreds more to each list, and some foods can probably be cross-listed. Since tastes and attitudes about food and beverages are highly individual, there are no right or wrong answers. Trust your own experience.

When you look through these lists, you may wonder, "What about balanced nutrition?" If you're able to eat food from the four food groups (see page 113) regularly your morning sickness is probably very manageable, and that's great. These lists of foods have been compiled to help the many women who are violently ill for long periods and need a fresh approach to finding foods and beverages they can keep down.

Consider those old stories men tell of midnight drives to find pickles and ice cream—what foods could be more dissimilar? Analyze both and see what characteristics emerge. Pickles are low in calories, have a high water content, are high in salt, potassium, and fiber; they have a distinct pungent aroma of vinegar, spices, and often garlic and dill. Ice cream is high in calories, has a lower water content but is a "solid liquid" of sorts; it's high in fat, low in salt, and potassium, and its aroma is often mild, partly because it's cold. Nutritionally, pickles and ice cream are not the least bit similar; but each can serve a purpose.

Again, your choice of foods and beverages can help to prevent potentially serious dehydration. Remember, though, that once your morning-sickness crisis is over, eating a balanced diet is critical. (My definition of a balanced diet takes into consideration the starting weight of a woman. See the tables starting on page 177; see also Chapter 12.)

By the way, grocery shopping can be another occasion for dread when you have morning sickness. You may be able to supply a list to the store and have an employee shop for you. (Some areas still have smaller stores that will accept telephone orders and deliver the groceries.) You'll need a preapproved check cashing card so that you can write out the exact charges beforehand (and don't forget to tip the employee). You may not get exactly what you would have chosen for yourself, but that gamble may be well worth taking.

The following lists of foods that many women find useful were compiled from my interviews over the past five years with women who had morning sickness.

Your preferences may change from time to time. It may be useful to write down the changes and date them; this information could show a trend when lots of variables come together. For example, when the weather changes from cold and brisk to hot and humid, in what direction do your food choices shift? Sharing your experiences with other women may unearth a lot of similarities.

SALTY

Mashed potatoes with salt and parmesan cheese
Noodles with salt or grated cheese
Thin slices of ham
Thin slices of cheese
Grilled cheese sandwich
Grilled ham and cheese sandwich
Baked potato with cheese sauce and bacon bits
Ham and cheese with mustard
Tuna fish
Tomato juice
V-8 juice
Bloody Mary mix (minus the alcohol)
Salted popcorn
Potato chips
Pretzels
Nacho chips
Macaroni and cheese
Quiche
Hot dog
Relish
Ketchup
Cheeseburger
Vegetable soup
Tomato soup
"String" cheese
Cheese spread
Cooked baby pasta (pastina) with salt and parmesan cheese
Instant or regular grits with salt and cheddar cheese
Gatorade (may not taste salty but has a fair amount of
     sodium in it)
Sausage
Bacon
"Cup 'o Noodles"
Cheese curls

Green apple (generally Granny Smith) sprinkled with salt
Anchovies
Caviar
Cheese and steak submarine sandwich
Deviled ham on crackers
Pickles

Cross out "no/never" items and add other favorite salty foods here.

_____

_____

_____

_____

BITTER/TART/SOUR

Pickles
English marmalade
Lemonade
Extra-sour lemonade
Lemonade mousse (see Recipes)
Whiskey sour mix (no alcohol)
Daiquiri mix (no alcohol)
Margarita mix (no alcohol)
Bloody Mary mix (no alcohol)
Grapefruit juice
Grapefruit juice with salt on the rim of the glass
Tom Collins mix (tonic, no alcohol)
Quinine (tonic) water
Tea (without milk or sugar)
Lemon wedges
Frozen lemon wedges
Frozen lime wedges
Frozen orange wedges
Fresh blueberries
Chinese plums
Tomato paste

Fresh cranberries
Sour apples
Concord grapes (jelly variety)
Lime juice sprinkled on apples
Limes
Rose's Lime Juice (mixed with water)
Tamarinds
Sauerkraut
Salsa
Mustard (try different kinds)

Again, cross out "no/never" items and use the space below to write additional items.

_____

_____

_____

EARTHY/YEASTY

Brown rice
Mushrooms
Herbs such as thyme and marjoram
Mushroom soup
Sautéed mushrooms
Miso soup
Cream of potato soup
Pumpernickel bread
Black Russian rye bread
Bran cereal
Wheat germ
Coarse-cut English or Irish oatmeal
Avocado
Spinach
Caesar salad (omit the raw egg in the dressing)
Baked potato
Mushroom pizza
Root beer

Cola
"Brown cow" (half milk and half cola)
Cheese bread
Ripe banana
Sourdough bread
Brie cheese
Boursin cheese
Raisin toast
Lemon-flavored Portuguese sweet bread
Finnish coffee bread (with cardamom seeds)
Rusks (a form of dried biscuit)
Hot-and-sour soup
Rice pilaf
Hummus
Borscht
Tofu
Ricotta cheese
Yogurt cheese
Blue cheese
Limburger cheese
Gouda cheese
Asparagus
Broccoli
Cauliflower
Brussels sprouts
Marinated mushrooms
Marinated artichokes
Bean burrito
Nuts
Smoked oysters
Clams (cooked and from inspected sources only)
Sardines
Mussels (cooked and from inspected sources only)
Pâté
Homemade hot cocoa
Sunflower seeds
Nut butters (cashew, peanut)
Mugwort soba (Japanese buckwheat pasta with mugwort leaf)
Lox

Cross out "no/never" foods and add other choices below.

CRUNCHY

"Potato crunchies" (see Recipes)
Baked potato skins
Celery sticks
Diced celery, chopped walnuts, and whole cranberries in gelatin salad (see Recipes)
Carrot sticks (to increase crunch and/or water content, soak them in cold water for an hour or two before eating)
Raw zucchini
Radishes
Lettuce
Crisp bacon
Fresh fruit cup
Fresh apple (red or green)
Cantaloupe
Honeydew melon
Fresh strawberries
Fresh blueberries
Pomegranates
Watermelon
Pears
Grapes
Potato chips
French fries
Cheese curls
Pretzels
Nuts
GORP (good old raisins and peanuts)
M&M's
Cucumbers
Pickles
Cherry tomatoes

Egg rolls
Sauerkraut on a hotdog
"Corndogs"
Taco shells
Matzo crackers

Cross out foods from the above list which are "no/never" and add other choices below.

_____

_____

_____

BLAND

Mashed potatoes
Rice
Egg noodles
Custard
Vanilla pudding
Tapioca
Cream of wheat
Cream of rice
Oatmeal
White toast
Plain crackers
Vanilla wafers
Matzo crackers
Fortune cookies
Pancakes
Cottage cheese
Plain yogurt
Vanilla yogurt
English muffins
Egg and plain bagels

Bland food is often thought of as the "white, yellow, and tan food group." Several foods in this group are staple items in our usual diet, like potatoes, rice, and noodles. These days more people are buying prepackaged, prepared noodles, rice, and potatoes to save time. These tend to cost more and contain more salt and MSG and fewer nutrients. There is an economical, convenient, and nutritious alternative to prepackaged starches: cook ahead and freeze.

If you don't already have a microwave oven, now is a good time to consider buying a no-frills model. However, if a microwave is not in your budget, you (or someone else in your house) can still do bulk starch cooking. To reheat these foods, use a double-boiler or slow oven (about 275 °F). Don't boil the frozen foods in the plastic bags in which they were frozen unless they're designed for that purpose. The average "freeze and store" plastic bag is not strong enough to withstand boiling water and may disintegrate either in the water or when removed, possibly causing burns. If you're using a microwave, be sure to get "microwaveable" bags. A toaster oven is also very useful for reheating food.

Mashed potatoes: Buy a five-pound bag of non-baking potatoes. If possible, have someone else peel and cook them all at once. Drain them and mash, adding the usual milk, margarine or butter, and seasonings. Line small custard dishes or measuring cups with plastic "zippered" sandwich bags. Scoop out ¾-cup servings and place in bags. Squeeze all the air out and seal. Date each portion. Put all individual packages on a 9-by-12-inch cookie sheet to quick-freeze. When the packages are hard, put them all in one large plastic airtight freezer box or large plastic bag. Later, simply pull one out of the freezer, empty into a microwaveable custard dish, and heat in the microwave about 1 minute on high. For variety add grated cheese when reheating. Add some low-fat milk slowly, stir with a fork, and reheat, and you've got instant cream of potato soup. Frozen mashed potatoes last about four weeks in the freezer.

Noodles: Cook a two-pound box. Drain and toss with a small amount of margarine to prevent sticking. Fill Ziploc bags with ¾-cup servings, squeeze out the air, date, and freeze. Frozen noodles keep about four weeks in the freezer. To use, reheat as above.

Rice: Cook two pounds (or more) according to package directions. Drain well. Divide into small freezer bags as directed above, squeeze out the air, date, and freeze. Frozen rice will keep well for four weeks in the freezer. Reheat as above.

If you want to make up a month's supply of basic cooked starch side dishes, do the potatoes, rice, and noodles in one day. Save pot washing time by cooking the rice first. As the rice is cooling, add water to the empty pot to boil for the noodles. The small bit of rice starch left in the pot won't make a difference.

Cook the noodles according to the directions on the package while dividing the cooked and cooled rice for the freezer. Once the rice strainer is empty, the noodles are probably ready to rinse and drain. After draining, put the noodles back into the large pot and toss with a bit of margarine to prevent sticking. Empty the noodles back into the strainer to cool. Then proceed with the packaging.

Add more water to the cooking pot to cook the potatoes. Once the potatoes are cooked and drained, mash them in the same pot. (One cautionary note: there are smells attached to cooking even these bland foods. The boiling water and vapors carry small amounts of starch molecules which have distinctive aromas. Even these mildest of aromas can trigger an episode of nausea. Be sure any cooking is done with opened windows and the exhaust fan on high speed.)

Hot cereal: Making a large batch of hot cereal at one time saves both time and money. Use the conventional oatmeal or hot cereal of your choice. Make six servings. When cool, refrigerate. To use, simply scoop out a single serving in a bowl, cover with plastic wrap, and microwave. Thin the hot cereal with milk for a satisfying, quick "pick-me-up" drink. Individual portions of oatmeal can also be successfully frozen in individual plastic containers or freezer bags. Thaw and reheat in the microwave or in a double-boiler.

SOFT

French toast (syrup optional)
Mashed potatoes
Rice
Noodles
Ice cream
Custard
Canned peaches and pears
Grilled cheese sandwich
Tortellini
Stuffed baked potatoes
Cream of wheat

Cream of rice
Pancakes
Yogurt
Cottage cheese
Canned fruit
Angel-food cake
Pound cake
Pudding
Danish pastry

Cross out foods which are "no/never" and add other choices below.

_____

_____

SWEET

Candy
Cake
Canned fruit
Ice cream
Sherbet
Dried fruit
Sugared cereal
Jam
Jelly
Syrup
Flavored instant hot cereal

Cross out "no/nevers" above and add favorites here.

_____

_____

FRUITY

Fresh fruit
Fruit in cereal
Jam on toast

Grilled ham and pineapple sandwich
Peanut butter and jelly sandwich
Canned fruit
Popsicle
Fruit leather
Dried fruit
Fruit blintz
Fruit compote

Cross out "no/never" foods and add any other favorites here.

_____

_____

WET

Seltzer
Tonic
Milk
Milkshake
Juice
Juicy fresh fruit
Slush
Pureed fruit
Water (see note below)
Thick and cold liquids (see description and instructions for
use for Thicken Up in Recipes)

Most women complain that their tap water has a funny taste or smell. Sometimes it's caused by algae that grow in the summer in the local reservoir, or by sulfur or chlorine. It might also be caused by metals which leak from old pipes or plastic components from newer synthetic pipes. Women in a queasy crisis often have more success with specific bottled waters.

Use this space to note more favorite wet items.

_____

_____

DRY

Crackers
Bread
Toast
Cookies
Cereal
Dried fruit
Beef jerky
Dried beef
Thai tea (see note below)
Freeze-dried ice cream (available in large science museums, at sporting goods/camping supply stores, or from the National Air and Space Museum in Washington, D.C.)

Not many liquids produce a "dry" sensation, but Thai tea seems to be one of them. If you don't have Thai tea but want to try something similar, simply add one teaspoon of vanilla to a cup of hot regular tea.

Write favorite dry foods here.

_____

_____

SPICY

Ginger ale
Homemade Ginger Ale (see Recipes)
Gingerbread
Gingerbread cookies
Salsa
Chili peppers
Hot dipping sauce
Tabasco
Seafood cocktail sauce
Guacamole

Curry
Cinnamon toast
Spices of any kind

Write favorite spicy foods in the space below.

_____

_____

HARD

Hard candy
Rusks
Biscotti
Crackers
Toasted bagel
Popsicles
Fresh fruit, (apple, pear, peach)
Dried fruit
Nuts
Beef jerky
Frozen chocolate chips
Frozen jelly beans
Ice chips
Frozen fruit-juice chips

Write favorite hard foods in the space below.

_____

_____

HOT

Just-cooked foods
Foods heated in a microwave
Hot liquids (if you drink tea, you may have more success if
it's tea piping hot rather than lukewarm)

Baked fruit
Freshly baked custard and pudding
Instant hot cereal
Spicy foods

Write favorite hot items here.

_____

COLD

Frozen desserts
Yogurt
Ice cream
Sherbet
Frozen fruit pops
Leftover chicken legs
Potato salad
Tortellini salad
Fruit soup
Iced tea
Iced herbal tea (in moderation due to unresolved
    controversy about the exact ingredients in many teas)
Lassi (Indian salty yogurt drink) (see Recipes)
Milkshake
Fruit shake
Chocolate milk
Strawberry-flavored milk
Leftover refrigerated pizza
Mousse
Frozen grapes
Pickles

Write favorite cold foods and beverages here.

_____

PUNGENT/AROMATIC/SPICY

Hot mustard sauce
Ginger

Ginseng tea (in moderation)
Mint tea (hot or cold)
Licorice
Anise
Rosemary
Garlic
Dill
Cinnamon
Other herbs and spices

List any favorite foods and beverages which come to mind in this category.

_____

_____

_____

Sick-Day Meal Plans

A few sick-day meal plans using the previous lists are provided here as examples only. I don't insist that you eat exactly in this fashion, particularly if you can tolerate other, more nutritious foods. A daily guide to more healthful eating can serve as a goal when your crisis is under control. Also note that food tastes are purely subjective. Feel free to recategorize each food into your own compartments.

SICK-DAY MEAL PLAN (SALTY)

7 A.M. (or first meal of the day) 8 salted soda crackers, matzos, or pretzels
8 A.M. 6 potato chips
9 A.M. ½ cup Gatorade
10 A.M. ½ sliced green apple, sprinkled with coarse salt
11 A.M. 4 or 5 cheese curls or ½ stick beef jerky

Noon ½ cup cooked pasta with 1 tablespoon grated parmesan cheese

1 P.M. ½ cup Gatorade or nonalcoholic Bloody Mary mix

2 P.M. 6 to 8 potato chips

3 P.M. ½ cup mashed potatoes with grated cheese

4 P.M. ½ cup chicken noodle soup

5 P.M. ½- or 1-ounce thinly sliced American cheese on a salted rice cake

6 P.M. 4 or 5 thinly sliced cucumbers, marinated in white vinegar and salt. Eat the thoroughly washed skins if possible for the fiber. Or try a few pickles.

7 P.M. ½ cup cooked pastina with salt added. (Cook the pastina in half water and half milk to add a bit more nutrition.)

Repeat any of the above as desired.

SICK-DAY MEAL PLAN (TART/BITTER/SOUR)

7 A.M. (or first meal of the day) 1 or 2 lemon sour balls

8 A.M. ¼ cup lemon pie filling with extra lemon rind or juice added

9 A.M. ¼ cup lime juice mixed with ¼ cup seltzer

10 A.M. ½ pomegranate

11 A.M. ½ cup (nonalcoholic) whiskey sour mix

Noon ½ cup frozen grapes rolled in "lime sugar" (see Recipes)

1 P.M. ½ cup "Charger" (see Recipes) or ½ cup tonic water

2 P.M. 1–2 tablespoons seafood cocktail sauce with lemon wedges and 1 or 2 (or more) freshly cooked shrimp

3 P.M. ½ cup homemade lemonade

4 P.M. ¼ turkey sandwich with tangy mustard

5 P.M. ½ cup lime pudding (adjust with extra lime juice) or a piece of key lime pie

6 P.M. ½ cup homemade cranberry juice

7 P.M. 1 or 2 gingersnaps, with low-fat ricotta or cottage cheese on top, sprinkled with nutmeg or ginger

8 P.M. Repeat any of the above as desired. Continue munching until bedtime.

SICK-DAY MEAL PLAN (BLAND)

7 A.M. (or first meal of the day) 4 unsalted oyster crackers
8 A.M. ½ egg matzo cracker
9 A.M. ½ cup instant cream of wheat or grits with milk
10 A.M. ½ ripe banana blended with ½ cup milk to make a milkshake
11 A.M. ¼ cup applesauce
Noon ½ cup quick pineapple yogurt blender pudding (see Recipes), or substitute canned pears for pineapple
1 P.M. ½ cup apricot nectar
2 P.M. ½ cup instant hot rice
3 P.M. ½ cup homemade tapioca or rice pudding
4 P.M. ½ cup fine-curd cottage cheese with ¼ cup diced guava added
5 P.M. ½ cup cream of potato soup, hot or cold
6 P.M. 1-inch square of noodle kugel (see Recipes)
7 P.M. 3 animal crackers and ½ cup warm milk (add vanilla to milk for a change)
8 P.M. 2 tablespoons whipped ricotta cheese on ½ cup warmed applesauce

Repeat any items as desired.

SICK-DAY MEAL PLAN (CRUNCHY)

7 A.M. (or first meal of the day) 3 melba toasts or 1 rice cake
8 A.M. ½ cup freshly sliced apple and ½ ounce cheddar cheese
9 A.M. ½ cup watermelon cubes
10 A.M. ½ cup wheat and fruit cereal with ¼ cup milk
11 A.M. 2 oatmeal raisin nut cookies
Noon ½ cup frozen grapes
1 P.M. ½ cup Gazpacho, hot or cold
2 P.M. 1 cucumber and watercress sandwich (very thin bread)

3 P.M. ¼ cup GORP (good old raisins and peanuts) or ¼ cup homemade granola with ¼ cup milk

4 P.M. 3 or 4 mandarin orange slices with slivered almonds and a leaf of Boston or Bibb lettuce

5 P.M. ½ bacon, lettuce, and tomato sandwich on toast

6 P.M. ½ cup Waldorf salad (see Recipes) with ¼ cup cottage cheese mixed in

7 P.M. ½ cup mild (homemade) chicken broth with ¼ cup chopped bok choy and ½ cup julienned carrots, cooked al dente, added

8 P.M. Repeat anything as desired.

SICK-DAY MEAL PLAN (SWEET)

7 A.M. (or first meal of the day) 2 shortbread or sugar cookies

8 A.M. 1-inch square noodle kugel (see Recipes)

9 A.M. ½ cup grape juice

10 A.M. 1 slice raisin toast with cinnamon sugar on top

11 A.M. ½ cup cherry mousse (see Recipes)

Noon 1 or 2 yogurt–cottage cheese pancakes, topped with Lyle's Golden Syrup or maple syrup

1 P.M. ½ cup cherry Gatorade or chocolate milk

2 P.M. ¼ to ½ cup raspberry or orange sherbet

3 P.M. ½ cup thawed frozen strawberries with juice and a ladyfinger

4 P.M. 1 small slice "easy refrigerator" pie (see Recipes)

5 P.M. ½ cup peach milkshake (3 peach halves blended with ¼ cup milk)

6 P.M. ½ cup baked "flan" (see Recipes)

7 P.M. ½ cup cranberry (sweetened) or apricot juice

8 P.M. 1 or 2 pieces of dried fruit

Continue nibbling as desired.

SICK-DAY MEAL PLAN (EARTHY)

7 A.M. (or first meal of the day) 1 whole-grain rice cake
8 A.M. ½ cup muesli and ¼ cup milk
9 A.M. 4 or 5 macadamia nuts
10 A.M. ½ Portuguese pancake with lemon curd
11 A.M. ½ cup maple tofu ice cream (see Recipes)
Noon Sautéed mushrooms over wheat toast
1 P.M. ¼ cup avocado whip (see Recipes)
2 P.M. ¼ cup prune juice or ½ cup prune whip (see Recipes)
3 P.M. 1 piece pumpkin cheese pie or ½ cup pumpkin custard (see Recipes)
4 P.M. 1 2-inch piece rice-carrot casserole (cold or hot) cut in thin slices (see Recipes)
5 P.M. ½ cup lemon and brown rice chicken casserole (see Recipes)
6 P.M. ½ cup buttermilk-fruit soup (see Recipes)
7 P.M. 1 tbsp. pâté or liverwurst on rye crackers
8 P.M. 1 or 2 sardines on ½ slice oatmeal toast

Eat more of the same as desired.

Your taste buds will most likely cry out for a variety of flavors throughout the day, and you'll mix and match foods from all of these lists. When you make a chart, you'll probably find that particular foods and beverages will predominate at the nadir and zenith of your nausea cycle. What's important is to find foods that work and map or chart them accordingly. After a cycle or two, this recorded information will most likely show a pattern and help you to predict which foods will may work for you.

CHAPTER 6

Noses:
Regular and Premium

My practice has convinced me that most of the physical complaints of morning sickness begin with the nose, thanks to the influence of pregnancy hormones. This chapter examines the role of odors in triggering the nausea and vomiting of morning sickness. Once you understand these connections you'll have more control of your own well-being.

The function of the nose is to filter and warm air with each breath. For the developing fetus as well as the mother, oxygen (transferred by the lungs to the blood) is needed to properly metabolize food. In the course of metabolism, the waste products of carbon dioxide are exhaled through the mouth and nose. During pregnancy a woman takes in more breaths per minute. One hormone that is believed to be responsible for increasing the respiration rate is estrogen.

Estrogen is also thought to enhance the sense of smell. Nausea, too, is said to increase sensitivity to odors. Although an enhanced sense of smell is really a benefit (it can protect you—and your baby —against dangers ranging from spoiled food to fire), the drawback is nausea.

Let's face it—smells are ubiquitous. They're connected with people; they lurk in your household and workplace; they're part of the outdoors.

Once you've figured out which smells trigger the nausea of morning sickness, you may or may not be able to take evasive actions. Everyone in your office will probably agree that the city garbage heap half a mile away means the windows can't be opened when the wind is blowing from that direction. Everyone may not agree that the smell of sludgy coffee cooking away all morning in the pot constitutes a major health hazard.

Some of the smells that tend to trigger morning sickness are more obvious than others. Women who live in large housing complexes complain about the cooking smells from each apartment—in winter, when closed windows keep in the odors, and in summer, when heat and humidity trap food smells in hallways. For some of the women I have counseled, the only solution is to find another place to live for a while. Some smells are more subtle, like the odor of stale cardboard boxes in kitchen cupboards. For the most part, trigger smells are very ordinary and are ignored by the average person.

Some sources of odors that are troublesome for women with morning sickness are listed below. Consider these lists a place to begin; use a notebook to record other specific smells that are triggers for you. Don't forget to share your list with other mothers-to-be.

The head. Your hair needs to be shampooed regularly, as it produces oils which can trap odors from food and smoke. Some hairstyles, such as once-a-week French twists and cornrows, may not be the best idea at this time, since they're shampooed less often. Shampoos, cream rinses and conditioners, hair sprays, and home permanents also contribute perfume smells.

The face. Aftershave and men's colognes often top the trigger list. Moisturizing lotions and makeup can also set off bouts of nausea.

The mouth. Everybody's breath has some odor, and depending on what you or your companions have eaten and your general physical health and oral hygiene, breath can seem unusually powerful to you when you're coping with morning sickness. Alcohol, coffee, and cigarettes on the breath are generally considered the worst. Dentures can emit odors, too.

Worried about being crude or insensitive, many pregnant women learn to simply hold their breath. But if your family's or friends' breaths are causing episodes of nausea and vomiting, you need to find a way to discuss the problem, perhaps by sharing this book.

The hands. Some chemical and food smells seem to become

permanently embedded in skin. A cook who chops onions and garlic all day can attest to this, as can a mechanic whose hands smell of grease. Rubbing the hands and fingers with lemon juice elminates strong food odors; a gritty hand-soap powder helps get rid of grease smells, or, if its smell doesn't bother you, Avon Skin-so-Soft works well, too.

Underarms. Besides the number-one problem of poor hygiene, the perfumes added to deodorants sometimes add insult to injury. A new unscented deodorant may help.

Feet. Shoes can become moldy and musty. Synthetic linings in inexpensive shoes and sneakers are more likely to make feet hot and sweaty. Some people take their shoes off under their desks—but for the pregnant woman, out of sight is not out of mind. If the person whose feet or shoes bother you is a family member, suggest deodorant insoles. Dirty, damp, and smelly socks sometimes lurk under a bed or other bedroom furniture. Get them into the wash immediately. More frequent or thorough foot washing or the use of foot powder may help.

Clothing. Wash clothes promptly after wearing them. Remember that clothes worn when cooking or where people are smoking pick up these odors. Some dry cleaners cut costs by not changing their cleaning fluids regularly; if your clothes don't come back smelling quite clean, mention it to the cleaner.

The kitchen. Kitchen curtains hold cooking odors and should be washed frequently in mild soap. Over time, kitchen walls also collect a thin film of grease from cooking. To create a relatively aroma-free kitchen, have someone sponge down all surfaces, including the ceiling. Be sure the cleansing solution is fairly diluted and has no added perfume—you don't want to replace one odor with another which may be just as offensive. Baking soda and warm water make a neutralizing rinse after a thorough wipe-down.

To wash her kitchen floor, one of my clients added several fresh cut-up lemons to a bucket of warm water.

Your tap water may smell funny to you, although that doesn't necessarily mean there's anything wrong with it. If the odor bothers you, try bottled water.

Many stores now offer customers a choice between paper and "biodegradable" plastic bags. Some of the biodegradables smell like burnt rubber, which may provide another irritant.

Check the pans under your stove burners for food spills. Ovens overdue for cleaning can emit rancid grease smells, especially when the heat is on.

Keep the refrigerator clean. Toss out any leftovers more than four days old—not only do leftovers lose their flavor and some nutritional value, but dangerous bacteria begin to accumulate. If possible, have someone else clean the inside of the refrigerator and wash and dry all the trays and drawers thoroughly. Don't forget the freezer. Even if your refrigerator is frost-free, you may find nearly prehistoric food in the far corners. Check for any poorly wrapped foods, since they can impart flavors to the ice cubes. Once the freezer and refrigerator are clean, put a new box of baking soda in both and extra boxes in the vegetable bins to absorb odor. Date the boxes and change them every few months. In between changes, shake up the contents so that a new layer of baking soda is on top. Use the old baking soda in water as a rinse to freshen up the shower or bathtub or to sprinkle down the kitchen and bathroom drains.

There's likely to be some smelly stuff in the kitchen drain. Instead of pouring corrosive chemicals down the pipes, a handy person might try wiggling a wire around to loosen any mysterious mass, which can then be flushed away with a generous stream of water. Some under-the-sink traps are easy to clean—just unscrew the large nut at the bottom. A few tablespoons of baking soda in the drain will freshen it up a bit. If you have a smelly garbage disposal, check the equipment manual for suggestions on cleaning and preventive maintenance. Try running some lemon rinds through the disposal. Don't forget to have someone check the dishwasher for hidden pieces of food chunks around the drain.

The bathroom. What goes for kitchen drains holds true for bathroom drains. Wipe down the tiles in the shower or tub with a mild detergent. (Never use bleach and ammonia together; the combination can produce deadly fumes.) Wipe surfaces instead of spraying, as sprays send extra chemicals into the air. Read labels and try to find a cleaner without propellants or perfumes, or use baking soda dissolved in water. Keep the shower curtain clean, too; wipe both sides with a fungicide and dry thoroughly. If the curtain is machine washable, wash it. Hang the curtain outside in the sun for a while if possible: the sun's ultraviolet rays will help kill any lingering mildew. Consider a new curtain or inexpensive liner.

You may want to avoid highly scented soaps. The hot water of a shower vaporizes the perfume in soaps. Soaps with "natural" orange, lemon, green apple, or cinnamon scents may be more refreshing. Discard or give away any perfumed bath cubes that may be hanging around your bathroom.

The Bedroom. Household aromas can creep into your room at any time. A draft dodger, one of those long fabric tubes, can keep smells from coming in under the door. Draft dodgers are easy to make and are also available in many mail-order catalogs.

Laundry detergents and fabric softeners can impart strong fragrances to nightclothes and bedding and can disturb your sleep. Try switching to an unscented detergent and softener. If you have to sleep away from home, take along your own pillow—or take two pillowcases to cut down on the odor of a strange pillow. Another defensive strategy is to put a favorite herbal tea bag inside a pillowcase. Use a familiar, mildly scented tea such as mint or lemon. Or use a favorite hard candy such as cherry, or a more pungent familiar smell like that of a cough drop.

The workplace. The main complaint of pregnant women may well be the collective coffeepot. Office coffeepots are notorious for sitting around all day and releasing the smell of scorched coffee, which by 11:15 A.M. is pretty much indistinguishable from the aroma of burning tires.

Workplace rest rooms are often not vented to the outside, and most have "air fresheners" in them which give off a fragrance designed to be stronger than the bathroom odors.

Many office buildings (and homes) are ill-ventilated in general, and more and more synthetic materials are being used for carpets, cabinets, countertops, and the like which give off chemical odors that may be particularly irksome to pregnant women.

CHAPTER 7

Other Times and
Other Places

Modern medicine, with all its advanced equipment, antibiotics, medications, and hydration techniques, has improved health outcome dramatically in the past fifty years. Long before hydration techniques were available, most ill people were treated with medicines made from herbs or plants, which still is the basis for over 40 percent of modern medicines. This was true for the woman affected with morning sickness.

Soranus, one of the first doctors to describe this client population, had a six-phase plan for treatment, heavily based on herbal concoctions.

Step 1: Don't eat if you're sick. Soranus reasoned that if not eating "cured" the nausea and vomiting of seasick sailors, it might be effective in treating morning sickness.

Step 2: If you do eat, eat easily digested foods, cold liquids, weak wine, and dry substances. Soranus also thought women should be carried in sedan chairs and should exercise both their bodies and voices to keep up their strength. Incidentally, sedan chairs look like tiny telephone booths carried on poles, which generally sway with the motion of the carriers!

Step 3: If the first two suggestions failed, one was to apply a mixture of freshly ground olives to the abdomen and bind with woolen bandages.

Step 4: Next, one would make the mixture of olives stronger.

Step 5: If that failed, one would add agents to this concoction: alum, aloe, saffron, pomegranate peel, oak galls, and barley meal to name a few.

Step 6: The woman was to have her extremities bound with tight bandages or be immersed in hot water.

How efficacious these plant based remedies were is not known. But during the Dark Ages, the use of herbs was considered pagan, so much of the experimentation was fairly secret. Monks and nuns, however, began to cultivate herbs in herb gardens, or physicks as they were then called, and there began the modern pharmacy. Herb crops were converted into potions and liquors which were dispensed to the sick and ailing.

One of the earliest persons to write about herbal cures was Nicholas Culpepper, a seventeenth century astrologer-physician. For vomiting, he suggested using bilberries, bistort, bucksborn, plantain, elder, and mint. To aid digestion, he prescribed lettuce, lovage, mint, black mustard, and rosemary. Stomach ailments were treated by adding marjoram, mint, black alder, broom, and caraway. For the pregnant woman, he recommended sniffing winter savory.

A Treatise of Midwifery, published in England in 1781 by Alexander Hamilton, recommended that the woman with morning sickness drink camomile tea. Two years later, Charles Elliot of Edinburgh and GGJJ Robinson of London recommended rhubarb in small doses along with strengthening bitters in their book *Outline of the Theory and Practice of Midwifery.*

Aristotle's Masterpiece: or the Secrets of Nature Displayed in the Generation of Man, published in 1801, recommended several herbal remedies for women with morning sickness, including tansy syrup, mallow, violets with sugar, and common oil. Other suggestions were "avoiding disturbing passions, loud clamours and filthy smells."

Reports from the middle 1700's give some sense of the consequences of this ailment. Kerking reported the first death in 1706. About a hundred years later, therapeutic abortion was presented as a cure for morning sickness. In 1853, the French medical society agreed with this suggestion. Ten years later, a Frenchman, Gueniot revealed these grisly statistics: 46 of 118 women died from morning sickness when all his known remedies for treatment failed.

In 1855 Charlotte Brontë succumbed to morning sickness after about eleven weeks of being ill. Her slow and agonizing decline is described in Elizabeth Gaskell's biography.

It is difficult to know the world-wide incidence of morning sickness as the incidences are not recorded. According to a source at the Office of International Statistics located in Hyattsville, Maryland, the World Health Organization reference, *WHO Annual Statistics 1991*, does not cover health codes past 469. Hyperemesis gravidarum has an international classification of disease (ICD) code of 643. It is highly unlikely that morning sickness does not exist, as in my interviews with tribal women in South Africa I learned many things. For example, most health problems are treated at the tribal level and the Xhosa women affected by nausea and vomiting of pregnancy are given bark water to drink. Contrarily, the Zulu women may eat a few balls of bland clay or chalk daily until the nausea and vomiting abate. Indian women in the South African region are reported to eat the sour tamarind fruit. There is evidence in the botanical literature of active ingredients in rosemary, thyme, sweet fennel, horehound, anise, and cumin that account for their use in treating morning sickness in other cultures.

As far as clay and chalk balls, each has different properties, depending on the region of the world where collected and color. For example, the red clay from Mississippi may have a high content of iron as well as aluminum, whereas gray colored clay from Georgia may have little iron but substantially more aluminum. A.R.P. Walker and colleagues from a prestigious South African university and research institute found a high percentage of black women who ate clay reported less severe nausea and vomiting associated with pregnancy. Unfortunately, the type of clay or earth eaten was not described. However, it was noted that the mixed race women ate soil and ice, the Indian women ingested soil and clay, though in lesser amounts, and the white women consumed some chalk and ice.

The field work of some notable geographers and anthropologists as John Hunter, Donald Vermeer, and Miles Richardson points to some new dimensions of earth eating, especially in cultural groups. Vermeer found, for example, that the clays eaten ritually are composed primarily of potassium and calcium. Ghanian women also have a superstition about not swallowing saliva, thinking that it makes them sicker. Women in the United States who have excess saliva report the same thing.

Some clay has been reported to have properties that resemble those of milk of magnesia. Thanks to its absorptive and neutralizing makeup, the use of activated charcoal was used for the treatment of gastric ulcers and other gastro-intestinal ailments in the 1920's. Medical reports can be found in such prestigious journals as *The Lancet,* the *Canadian Medical Journal,* and the *Hahnemannian Monthly.*

But there are cultural and religious attachments to geophagy, or the eating of earth, as noted by the team of geographers lead by John Hunter in 1989 as well as Miles Richardson and William Davidson as they visited the community of Esquipulas, Guatamala. Here clay is molded into religious figures called *panito del Senor* and blessed in the Shrine of the Black Christ, or *el Christo Negro.* This special clay is considered "cool" and is thought to relieve the discomforts of pregnancy, which are considered "hot." Clay of this region is of the smectite variety and contains calcium, which is easily stripped out, expands in fluid and is thought to reduce gastric acidity. Georgia clay, as I noted before, is higher in iron; white or gray clays are higher in other minerals. Clay eating has been reported to reduce excess salivation and altered taste and smell.

Anemia in pregnancy may be worsened by eating clay since it may reduce gastric acid secretions by absorption. A certain amount of gastric acid is needed to turn ferric iron into ferrous iron, the form the body uses to prevent anemia. Likewise, eating cornstarch, a dry, bland, odorless, and smooth source of calories, has been implicated in promoting iron-deficiency anemia, probably because it contains no nutrients except for calories.

Treatments for morning sickness in other cultures range from the use of herbal teas to the eating of dry clay or chalk-like substances. One woman from Barbados said she knew many women who would eat dry arrowroot starch and travel miles into the country to get a special clay. A woman from Trinidad said Enos, a relative of Alka-Selzter, was a popular treatment in her area. Another said some women would travel to a remote but pristine beach to drink sea water. An Indian woman remarked that her friends would simmer a blend of spices, predominantly anise, and drink the elixir.

Ginger has been used in several cultures to quell nausea. In most hospitals, ginger ale is a preferred beverage for nauseated patients. Eating lemons has been noted as a remedy for seasickness. In my clinical experience, I've observed a strange but real therapeutic effect of lemons. My clients can do whatever they wish with their fresh lemons. Some sniff them, others suck wedges plain, and some eat them sprinkled with salt. It is true that lemons are acidic and that repeatedly eating them may harm dental enamel, but so will vomitus and the lemon therapy never lasts long.

Then there is ice eating or pagophagia. Interestingly, this has been associated with iron-deficiency anemia, but women who eat ice for hydration are generally eating very little high nutrient food, simply because of nausea and vomiting. Many women are often slightly anemic before pregnancy and are unaware of it until seeing a doctor on a regular basis. The reason is often heavy monthly blood losses combined with marginal diets. So once a woman has morning sickness and sees her doctor, her anemia may have gotten worse. Whether one can blame eating ice on the anemia in pregnancy is questionable. Ice and water provide few nutrients but are vital to sustaining metabolic processes. One of my clients said the cold ice was the only thing that could reduce the feeling of fire in the back of her throat, the result of endless vomiting episodes. (See Chapter 9, page 77, foods with high iron.)

Besides eating different cultural "bandage foods," women in less developed countries are often more tied to a woman's network. When one member is unable to perform her usual duties, most of the others divide up and perform her tasks as a matter of course. Unfortunately, this sort of selfless camaraderie is lacking in highly sophisticated countries today.

CHAPTER 8

Morning Sickness Is Not in Your Head

In 1891, a German named Kaltenbach presented a paper before the Berlin Obstetrical Society which proclaimed that "the vomiting of pregnancy was usually a manifestation of neurosis, somewhat allied to hysteria and ready amendable to suggestive therapy."

This charge that morning sickness had a neurotic component led researchers (mostly men) to investigate every pregnant woman's pyscho-social-economic background. Someone had proposed that an unmarried woman shamed by her condition of pregnancy might be more inclined to vomit. However, marital status was found to have no bearing on the incidence of morning sickness. There was also a theory, since disproved, that the vomiting was a sign that the pregnancy was unwanted.

No one knows exactly what women with nausea and vomiting in early pregnancy were told by their obstetricians in the nineteenth and twentieth centuries. Since maternal mortality from morning sickness was significant, anxiety on the part of a pregnant woman might have been common. Acknowledging that even today in the best of circumstances, nausea can be relentless, the challenges for obstetricians before the advent of modern hydration therapy must have been monumental.

Anxiety among pregnant women was undoubtedly heightened by theories about deformities in children, outlined in 1832 by two French scientists, Etienne and Isidore Gregory St. Hilaire. These scientists voiced concern that hyperemesis gravidarum, the severest form of morning sickness, was the cause of fetal deformities.

Theoretical dialogue continued into the 1930's, 1940's and 1950's. In 1936, a study conducted by the German scientist H. Naujoks showed that about 16 percent of the children he studied with deformities had mothers who had been affected by hyperemesis gravidarum. In 1942, another study found that six of eleven mothers with vomiting in pregnancy bore deformed children, and in 1953 a scientist named Thalhammer established a relationship between vomiting in pregnancy and deformities. We now know that most women who experience the nausea and vomiting of morning sickness have healthy babies with no deformities.

We also know that there are many environmental and genetic factors to consider when evaluating birth defects and any relationship to the nausea and vomiting of early pregnancy. But the suspected link between the reported deformities and the common occurrence of nausea and vomiting seemed to be the driving force that led many scientists, like L. F. Hawkinson in the 1930's, to ponder the use of hormones to women with low estrogen levels in pregnancy and antiestrogens to women with high estrogen levels. In the early 1940's O. W. Smith, G. V. Smith and S. Schiller treated women affected with morning sickness with diethylstilbesterol (DES) daily and claimed success, relief of nausea and vomiting, in 70 percent of cases, while 26 percent showed "improvement." DES was a drug that later was shown to be associated with a high incidence of cervical cancer in the daughters of mothers who took this drug.

The pervasive Kaltenbach theory about morning sickness neurosis commentary influenced a great many clinicians. H.B. Atlee wrote in 1934 in the *Journal of Obstetrics and Gynecology of the British Empire* that pernicious severe vomiting was indeed a neurotic manifestation and he formulated a treatment program. He banned visitors to the patients for forty-eight hours, allowed no vomit bowl in the patient's room, allowed the patient to vomit in her bed, and instructed the nurse caring for the patient to take her time in changing the soiled linen and then feed the patient twenty minutes later. Another British researcher reported in 1945 that it was customary to send in the "most angry and foul-mouthed ward maid to clean up the mess."

In 1939 two other theories were put forward: Karl Menninger thought that vomiting in pregnancy was due to a "repudiation of femininity" and H. C. Hesseline believed "the vomiting was a form of self-punishment." In the same year, Menninger also wrote that the type of person most affected by hyperemesis was "well to do" or the intellectual college girl. He argued that the syndrome was not prevalent in Southern black women or the poor and uneducated. G. Gladstone Robertson, writing in 1946 in England's influential *Lancet* said that a high proportion of the women who suffered from nausea and vomiting in pregnancy were, at the times of their marriages, overly attached to their mothers and had some degree of sexual revulsion toward their husbands. He did not study the degree of maternal attachment or sexual revulsion outside the context of nausea and vomiting of pregnancy. Robertson noted that one-third of these women continued to be sick beyond the fifth month of pregnancy, whereas the majority two-thirds were sick six weeks or less.

In the early 1960's, Denys Fairweather from London used a health questionnaire, the Cornell Medical Index, along with the Minnesota Multiphasic Personality Inventory to conclude that these forty-four women had a "marked association with a hysterical personality." Fairweather went on to say that there was little doubt that psychiatric factors must be implicated in 75 to 80 percent of the cases of severe morning sickness.

Over the years, research interest in the area of morning sickness has been sparse. At least two studies have been conducted which involved a trial of vitamin B6 vs. a placebo. In the Iowa study which involved 59 women at 9 weeks gestation in 1991 it was concluded that the women with less severe nausea and vomiting seemed to benefit by the supplement. In an earlier British study done in the middle 1980's, data from 180 pregnant women failed to show that additional vitamin B6 reduced symptoms. Caveats about vitamin B6 abound, however. A study published in the *New England Journal of Medicine* in 1983 indicated that megadoses of vitamin B6 might have been responsible for loss of nerve sensation in seven people who took the supplement for a long period of time.

The 1989 recommended dietary allowance for vitamin B6 in pregnancy is 2.1 mg/day, down slightly from the 1980 recommendations. Vitamin B6 can be obtained from eating a variety of protein foods, grains and cereals as noted from this chart.

Recent interest in Oriental medicine has prompted an Italian research group to investigate wrist acupressure, using Seabands on either the right or left wrist and measuring severity of nausea and vomiting. The data again show some benefit to a small group of women. But neither of these studies discuss the influence of smells, foods desired and eaten, and several other important factors.

One recent milestone study, conducted by Priscilla Bolte in July 1989 from Boston, has yet to be incorporated into teaching texts. Bolte systematically explored nausea and vomiting and foods eaten by clients by degree of relief conferred. After interviews with 133 women, she concluded that there was no universal cure, and that the key is individual observation and exploration.

Some professional reference books speculate that reduced levels of niacin and pyridoxine (vitamin B6) may be responsible for some neurological signs and symptoms of anxiety, depression, and thought disorders which are seen in cases of malnutrition and extreme weight loss. Some people feel that this may also be the case with morning sickness as well. Others have mentioned that thiamine (vitamin B2) is reduced with poor intake and vomiting and speculate that taking in more B1-rich foods should be helpful.

Vitamin B6 Content of Some Foods

Food	Calories	Serving Size	mg of Vitamin B6
Lean Beef	230	3 oz	.21
Broiled Cod	160	3 oz	.28
Cream of rice	240	1 cup	.07
Instant oatmeal (fortified)	100	¾ cup	.74
Cooked spaghetti	200	1 cup	.05
Fresh strawberries	45	1 cup	.09
Cooked plantain	180	1 cup	.37
Cooked broccoli	45	1 cup	.22
Mashed potatoes w/milk	160	1 cup	.49

One prenatal nutrition reference supports the theory that nausea and vomiting may be caused by irritation of the vagus nerve from the direct action of the hormone estrogen. The vagus nerve is responsible for swallowing, taste, and gastrointestinal stability as it sends messages between parts of the brain to the stomach, heart, esophagus, and intestines. I interviewed a woman in 1990 who was told by her doctor that her "all-day sickness" was due to pressure on her vagal nerve. Besides vomiting, she experienced diarrhea. She found moderate relief in eating very small solid meals, alternating fluids in between and lying down for short periods of time after eating or drinking anything.

C H A P T E R 9

Special Concerns

For many women the nausea and vomiting of morning sickness are occasional, not continual, and are limited to the first trimester of pregnancy. However, women with severe and extended morning sickness are at risk for other problems besides poor nutrition:

    inadequate weight gain
    marginal fluid consumption
    constipation
    anemia
    tooth and gum problems
    irritation of the throat and nose
    early satiety and overeating
    muscle loss from prolonged bed rest
    heightened physical discomfort

The impact of each of these can be minimized with increased awareness and by making better food choices when possible. Each of these factors, while related to your overall diet, is important for special reasons.

Inadequate weight gain

All women don't need to gain the same amount of weight during pregnancy. The charts starting on page 177 provide a suggested rate of gain, which depends on your prepregnancy weight. An underweight woman needs to try to gain more weight than a woman who started her pregnancy overweight. However, weight gain in the latter part of pregnancy seems to be more important because the fetus is growing so quickly.

Many women who lose weight in the early months make it up once morning sickness subsides. Some women do not lose weight at all, despite episodes of vomiting. Becoming anxious about weight gain, or the lack thereof, simply generates more stress.

In understanding weight loss, you should be aware that different women have a wide range of total body water. For a woman at her desirable body weight before pregnancy, about 57 percent of the weight is water if she's under eighteen years old and about 51 percent if she's eighteen to forty years old. An overweight person may have a smaller proportion of water in her body, as there is less water in fat tissue. This means that when a leaner woman loses weight, the percentage of water lost will probably be greater compared to an overweight woman who loses weight.

Some doctors consider hospitalizing a woman with morning sickness once her weight loss reaches 5 percent of her body weight, so a leaner woman may be hospitalized sooner than her counterpart who is a few pounds heavier.

Marginal fluid consumption

Most people have a daily fluid need of 2.5 liters, which is 2.65 quarts. About two-thirds of the fluid requirement is obligatory—that is, the necessary and required amount of fluid needed daily to remove waste materials from the body in the urine. The body also needs fluid for the proper functioning of the gastrointestinal tract.

About one-third of the daily fluid you take in is lost through the lungs via breathing and through the skin as perspiration. To be safe, aim for eight to ten (eight-ounce) glasses of fluid a day. A way to keep track is to plan to drink two-thirds of a cup of fluid for every waking hour, which may be a chore if you're nauseated. To make it seem more manageable, try for a shot glass every ten minutes.

Normal fluid consumption for a healthy person comes from three basic sources:

1. Fluids ingested. This accounts for about 50 percent.

2. Foods consumed. Many foods contain a certain amount of fluid, and on average this accounts for slightly less than one quart.

3. Metabolism of food. Also called oxidation, this is a long, elaborate series of biochemical events which releases small amounts of water in the process. The water generated from metabolism accounts for about 14 percent of the daily total.

Water in the body is critical to maintaining health—for proper biological reactions to occur, to regulate body temperature, and to avoid constipation.

Choosing foods which contain plenty of water can prevent both constipation and dehydration. The following table shows how small differences in food choices can make a big difference in maintaining hydration. Foods with more fiber also help to prevent constipation (see the discussion below).

Note that food can lose water in preparation, such as by toasting.

Constipation

Five essential factors affect the moisture content of the feces:

fiber content of the diet
fluid consumption
regular daily exercise or activity
medication
tension and stress

The first two factors may be more obvious than the last three. Getting regular daily exercise, of course, depends on your overall well-being, which is certainly influenced by nausea and vomiting. Some medications designed to reduce the spasms in the stomach which propel food upward can also reduce intestinal peristalsis, the progressive waves of contraction and relaxation in the intestinal tract which move food through. When peristaltic action is reduced, intestinal matter moves more slowly than usual. The result is that more water can be reabsorbed from it, especially if fluid intake is low. While this helps maintain hydration, the stool becomes harder and bowel movements can become difficult.

Water and Fiber Contents of Some Foods

Type of Food	Serving Size (average)	Water Content (est., in tbsp)	Fiber Content (approx. in g)
White bread	1 slice	2	.5
White toast	1 slice	1	.6
Cracked-wheat toast	1 slice	1	1.4
Cracked-wheat bread	1 slice	1½	1.3
Mixed-grain bread	1 slice	2	1.6
Mixed-grain toast	1 slice	1	1.6
Soda crackers	8 squares	1	.7
Apple juice	½ cup	8	.1
Medium apple	2¾ in. diam.	8	3.4
Milk	8 oz	8	0
Lemon yogurt	8 oz	8	0
Oatmeal (quick)	1 package cooked	6	2.0
Cream of wheat	½ cup cooked	7	1.7
Mashed potato	½ cup	5	1.5
Boiled potato	5 oz	5	2.0
Baked potato	7 oz (large)	9	4.7
Gelatin dessert	½ cup	7	0.1
Gelatin-carrot salad	5 oz	8	1.1

Poorly managed tension and stress can cause gastrointestinal (GI) problems ranging from diarrhea to constipation. When the muscles in the GI tract are relaxed, the contents are moved along normally; tension can disrupt this process. The tension can be as subtle as not having your own bathroom available on demand, say when you're away from home or you have house guests.

When you have a choice among foods, select the one with both the most fiber and most fluid if possible. The following table points out the differences among some foods. Choosing the right one can make a substantial improvement in your nutrition.

At times it may be difficult for you to find foods which contribute both fiber and fluid to your diet. Severe cases of constipation, requiring manual disimpaction by a doctor, have been caused by serious morning sickness. Since disimpaction can be uncomfortable, embarrassing, and expensive, prevention is the best approach.

Anemia

Most anemias during pregnancy are caused by low iron consumption or previous excessive blood loss through menstruation. When you're newly pregnant, iron deficiency can take on new significance if your consumption of protein foods is low and your diet is high in carbohydrates.

Fluid, Fiber, and Iron Contents of Some Foods

Food	Portion	Fluid Content	Fiber Content (in g)	Iron Content (in mg)
Banana	1 medium	74% or 1/3 cup	2.3	.35
Apple	1 medium	84% or 1/2 cup	3.4	.25
Milk	8 oz	88% or 7/8 cup	—	.11
Broccoli	1 cooked spear	90% or 2/3 cup	5.5	1.51
Carrots	1/2 cup cooked	87% or 2/3 cup	2.7	.48
Chicken	3 oz baked	65% or 2 T	—	.30
Dynamite Drink	7 oz	83% or 5 3/4 cup	2.3	.68

Anemia often manifests itself as fatigue. Because of reduced amounts of iron, the blood can't carry as much oxygen to the body parts. Women, pregnant or not, who suffer iron-deficiency anemia are also less tolerant of cold. Getting adequate iron requires a concerted effort, as you'll see in the iron content table opposite.

As a point of reference, the prepregnancy daily allowance is 15 milligrams of iron. For pregnant women the daily allowance triples to 45 milligrams per day. Most pregnant women take prenatal vitamins with iron to meet their needs.

Prenatal iron supplements are often prescribed to prevent or resolve anemia. However, iron can be irritating to the stomach. Taking iron with food can reduce this problem, but if you're having nausea and vomiting, this may be difficult. Iron can also be constipating, especially if fiber and fluid intake are low.

If it's not possible to take an iron supplement every day, you should eat as many high-iron foods as possible. Although anemia may be a problem, most doctors and nutritionists believe it's most important to prevent dehydration. Sometimes it's not possible to solve all the problems at once, and setting priorities becomes critical.

Tooth and Gum Problems

What you regularly eat affects the health of your teeth. High-fiber and high-protein foods don't contain many carbohydrates, which if left on or around the teeth allow mouth bacteria to produce acids that can erode tooth enamel. During morning sickness, the foods which are best tolerated may not be the ones which promote dental health.

For a few days at a time your daily diet might include large amounts of crackers, rice, puddings, and yogurt drinks. It becomes even more important than usual to brush your teeth as frequently as possible to remove particles of sugars and starches.

However, many women find that brushing their teeth can become a trigger for vomiting. The motion, the smell of the toothpaste, and the toothbrush generating a gag reflex when it gets close to the back of the throat are all possible triggers.

If you look at the diagram of the tongue on page 181, you'll notice two small places marked "vagus nerve." The vagus nerve

Iron Content of Some Foods

Food	Portion	Iron (in mg)
Pork chop	3½ oz	3.9
Calf's liver	3½ oz	14.2
Chicken (white meat)	3½ oz	1.7
Egg	1 medium	1.0
Kidney beans	½ cup cooked	2.3
Peanut butter	2 tbsp	0.6
Swordfish	3½ oz	1.3
Clams	3½ oz	4.1
Oysters	3½ oz	6.6
Shrimp	3½ oz	1.8
Enriched bread	1 slice	0.6
Whole-wheat bread	1 slice	0.6
Bran flakes	1 oz	4.5
Enriched rice	1 cup cooked	1.8
Oatmeal	¾ cup cooked	1.0
Prune juice	8 oz	3.0
Dried prunes	10 medium	2.1
Raisins	⅓ cup	1.0
Cooked peas	½ cup	1.6
Lima beans	½ cup	2.1
Cooked broccoli	1 spear, 6 oz	1.5
Baked potato	1 medium	0.7
Ovaltine	2 tbsp	4.0
Wheat germ	¼ cup	2.5
Cooked lentils	⅔ cup	2.1
Blackstrap molasses	1 tbsp	2.3
Tofu	3½ oz	2.3

has connections in many places in the body, and one major connection is to the stomach. It may be that brushing close to these
spots on the tongue sets up negative sensations. If switching brands

of toothpaste or trying tooth powder is not successful, try using salt or baking soda. If your gums are bleeding, as can occur in pregnancy, try to massage them with your fingers to stimulate circulation.

Or just brush with water. To help remove food particles, flossing is recommended. If you can't stand flossing right now, it may be useful to rinse your mouth several times a day with water. Since plain water is also high on the complaint list, try using naturally flavored water: For mint water, crush a handful of fresh mint leaves and put into the bottom of a large glass bottle. Fill with cold water and refrigerate. As water is used, replace to keep the bottle full. Change the mint leaves every other day. For lemon water, slice a whole lemon and put into a large glass bottle. Follow directions for mint water. Limes are another possibility, or try a combination of both.

Chewing lemons or limes helps settle some women's stomachs (and lemons and limes contain lots of vitamin C and potassium). However, acidic foods have been reported to sharply increase the rate of salivation. Increased saliva may lessen the possibility of damage to the dental enamel as a consequence of eating lemons and limes. At any rate, I've found that the period of lemon-eating is usually too short to be worrisome.

Saliva

Many women complain that excess saliva adds to their nausea. Saliva production is beyond conscious control. In fact, saliva normally bestows many benefits. It provides one of the first phases of the body's defense system because it helps to destroy bacteria in food. Saliva also helps to lubricate food, making swallowing easier. The production of saliva is controlled by the taste and smell centers of the cerebral cortex. Some medication given to try to control nausea and vomiting can also affect saliva production, which may influence a woman's unconscious choices of food.

Pregnancy hormones have been shown to change the composition of saliva enough to cause a difference in taste perception. Investigators have found that even distilled water can taste bitter. In the early weeks of pregnancy women often complain that various foods "just don't taste the same anymore." Women are relieved to learn that an actual physiological change has occurred and that this perception is not psychological.

Tasting food has a lot to do with saliva. The flavor components of foods and beverages are dissolved in saliva, which then washes over the taste buds. Humans can taste salt at a ratio of 1 to 400, sour at 1 part per 130,000, and bitterness at 1 part per 2 million. There is a protective message here. Since many of nature's bitter substances are associated with poisons, the ability to detect bitterness at this range was probably a matter of survival. Saliva is just another part of a survival scheme, although if at this point you are in the misery sequence of morning sickness, it may seem counterproductive.

In addition, saliva contains an enzyme, amylase, which is helpful in starch breakdown. One of the main components of saliva is bicarbonate, a "counter-agent" to lactic acid, which is produced by resident micro-organisms in the mouth, or hydrochloric acid, the major acid in the stomach. A high level of saliva with its corresponding high level of bicarbonate would also protect the teeth from the effects of gastric acid from the stomach which comes in contact with teeth during vomiting. Saliva also contains calcium, an effective buffer that minimizes calcium loss from the teeth. Dehydration, fear, and anxiety can reduce saliva production, as can some antinausea medications.

Interestingly, a difference in the rate of saliva flow has been demonstrated in a population of "eaters" and "non-eaters." In one experiment, "eaters"—a term used to describe persons with the eating disorder bulimia—were found to have significantly greater amounts of saliva than "non-eaters," or persons with anorexia. It may seem reasonable to postulate that some women with morning sickness may experience excessive saliva, or hyperptyalism, for the same reasons. Perhaps women who are more likely to vomit produce more saliva when compared to those who suffer nausea only. It's also possible that the extra saliva produced not only neutralizes the gastric acid from vomit in the mouth but also affords some measure of protection for dental enamel.

Wartime experience has shown that when food supplies are low people develop rituals with their food and have preoccupations and food thoughts constantly. Although women with morning sickness do not share the same stresses, there is an issue of food restriction. In my experience, women whose intake is limited because of the fear of exacerbating nausea and the potential of vomiting often have constant thoughts and dreams of food.

Close clinical experience and observation have demonstrated to me that the disposal of excess saliva is handled differently by women of different cultures. Some hospital personnel have long noted that women from lower socio-economic areas and/or the Caribbean area are more prone to spitting out excess saliva. It is not uncommon to find copious piles of soiled tissues at the bedsides of the average surburan patient whose chief complaint is nausea. One learns upon inquiry that the tissues are used for the disposal of saliva. Women with excess saliva, regardless of ethnicity or nationality, report that swallowing saliva by itself only adds to the sensation of nausea. Probably spitting into containers as opposed to using tissues has to do with habit. Persons who grew up with limited finances may not have had free access to tissues and therefore may not use them routinely. But many women complain of excess saliva regardless.

Irritation of the Throat and Nose

Some women are concerned by the throat irritation which accompanies vomiting. They may select less "scratchy" foods, like bread rolls. Many women report that orange juice is the most likely food item to be vomited through the nose, and they avoid it after the first occurrence. Eating the pulp from oranges seems to pose less of a problem. Eating ice chips seems to be a quick way to soothe a red, raw throat.

Early Satiety and Overeating

As difficult or impossible as it sounds, women with nausea and vomiting do overeat from time to time, generally between bouts of illness.

It takes time for the brain to appreciate the volume of food which is ingested when you eat quickly.

For the woman with morning sickness, "speed eating" can have deleterious consequences. Gastric distress may result in renewed episodes of vomiting. So, despite the internal signals that are being sent to hurry up and eat, it's important to take time, chew slowly, and stop eating when you begin to feel the least bit full. If in a little while your hunger still persists and your stomach feels stable, have another small meal. Learn to listen to stomach messages. Ignore pressure from family and friends to "have just one more bite" when the internal message is *"enough!"*

Other factors, such as fear and depression, can decrease gastric secretions and blood flow to the stomach, and this can delay stomach emptying. It's difficult to know how much worry and stress a woman with morning sickness is experiencing, which adds to the problem.

Muscle Loss from Prolonged Bed Rest

People on prolonged bed rest, whether twenty years old and suffering from skiing injuries or eighty-five with arthritis, lose both muscle and skeletal mass. Certainly a woman who spends the majority of her pregnancy in bed or off her feet falls victim to the weaknesses which accompany lost muscle strength. Rebuilding strength takes longer than losing it.

Be aware that muscle and bone wasting can be a consequence of any extended bed rest or inactivity. Sets of activities designed by registered physical therapists can help minimize long-term consequences of bed rest.

Heightened Physical Discomfort

People who are dehydrated often can't tolerate extremes of temperature, especially cold. Turning up the thermostat when you feel cold only serves to hasten fluid loss through the skin. A better alternative is to wear one or two pairs of absorbent cotton or wool socks (or cotton blend), cotton or silk long johns, and a long-sleeved T-shirt under ordinary clothes. And add a hat! Heat lost through the top of the head can amount to 40 percent.

Your choice of clothing also makes a difference in your overall level of comfort. Loose clothing permits a layer of air between the body and clothes to hold in warmth. Many pregnant women also find clothes that are snug around the waist annoying. If you're indoors, bundle up to be comfortable. Make sure the clothes you add are loose and bulky, not tight and confining.

If you've lost weight, you may become chilled more easily, as your body has lost some of its insulating layer of fat. When you feel cold, you may start to shiver. Shivering is actually an attempt on the part of the body to generate heat and uses up a fair number of calories, so conservation of your body heat is important. Another physiological response to being chilled is a contraction of thousands of muscles on the sebaceous glands. These glands then produce an oily insulating secretion which is thought to help retain heat and water. Some women wonder why they feel so sticky just from lying around when they're sick, and this may be part of the explanation.

You may find that breathing colder air is more comfortable, perhaps because it reduces the odors you can detect. However, if the environment is too cold, 68°F or less, the body uses more oxygen, and hence more calories, to produce heat. Several women have reported to me that a violent shiver in a cold environment, for example starting the car on a subzero winter morning, is enough to trigger a cycle of nausea and vomiting. If that turns out to be true for you, ask someone else to start and warm your car if possible.

Some women report their skin seems extra-sensitive, making skin contact unpleasant. One universal sign that nausea is beginning to escalate is a desire not to be touched.

Spending several hours a day in bed between "wrong-feeling" sheets can keep you from feeling rested. Pure cotton sheets are considered more comfortable, since they absorb body moisture better than polyester-cotton blends, and some women prefer the scratchier surface of natural cotton sheets as well. Experiment to see what works best. As far as bed linens go, women often say the more highly colored ones have more of a chemical smell, so try white sheets.

You may feel more rested if your mattress is turned and rotated. This is something that bedding manufacturers recommend to extend the life of the mattress, but few people do it regularly.

CHAPTER 10

Worst-Case Scenario: Being Hospitalized

According to American statistics, about one pregnant woman in 72 is hospitalized with severe morning sickness. This means that each year about 55,000 American women require hospitalization, most often due to dehydration. To prevent or delay hospitalization, some doctors perform intravenous hydration in their offices first. Other doctors' offices are either too busy or too small to provide this type of service.

The factors which affect your doctor's decision whether or not to admit you to the hospital include:

1. *Amount of weight loss.* If you're seriously dehydrated and unable to eat, weight loss will be obvious. If you receive intravenous fluids, the scales will show an immediate gain of a few pounds. This is water weight; every two pounds reflects about one quart of fluid. If your weight remains significantly below your prepregnancy weight as the weeks go on, your doctor will be concerned.

2. *Amount of weight loss compared to your desirable body weight.* If you were a bit overweight when you became pregnant, your doctor may wait a little longer before hospitalizing you, as long as your blood pressure and urine output are adequate. An overweight woman has extra fat mass that can be used for energy. Since no one knows when the nausea and vomiting of pregnancy will end, the physician uses his or her discretion to admit or to wait.

3. *Fainting.* A woman can put herself and others at risk when

she loses consciousness, even for a short time. Fainting is a sign of low blood pressure, resulting from low blood volume. This may be caused by vomiting or by inadequate consumption of liquids.

4. *Vomiting blood.* Vomiting blood may be caused by Mallory-Weiss tears, which occur when the tissues where the esophagus and the stomach join are torn. Dry heaves and violent and repeated retching can cause such tears. But vomiting blood can also be a sign of bleeding ulcers, which are life-threatening. A woman with a history of ulcers or gastritis may be more at risk for bleeding ulcers. Your physician needs to order tests to determine the cause and the significance of any vomiting of blood.

5. *Rib pain.* Violent retching and vomiting can strain rib muscles as well as fracture ribs. The pain from broken ribs can make breathing and sleeping difficult. Hospital care for a few days should speed recovery.

6. *Jaundice.* When the skin begins to take on a green or yellow cast, jaundice may be the cause. Jaundice is a symptom of a variety of diseases, some major and some minor. Jaundice results when bile cannot be excreted in the usual manner. Pregnancy-related digestive upsets can disturb the normal functioning of the gallbladder and bile release. When bile is retained in the gallbladder longer than usual, the pigments that make up its greenish color are absorbed into the rest of the body. Because jaundice is a warning sign of other potential complications, hospitalization, intravenous fluids, and observation are necessary.

7. *Physician's experience.* Before admitting a woman to the hospital, each physician exercises clinical judgment that depends on previous experience with cases of morning sickness.

Even if your morning sickness seems quite severe, you may not need to be admitted to the hospital. But should you be admitted, there are some things you need to know.

Admission

If you're admitted through an emergency room, the process may be slow. Emergency rooms function on the premise that the biggest disaster comes first. A pregnant woman who is vomiting will probably be considered less of an emergency than a car-crash victim. It's helpful if someone accompanies you, bringing an "air sickness" bag and a few cold, wet facecloths.

If you're admitted through the labor and delivery rooms, the immediate needs of women in active labor will take precedence. Once the paperwork is finished, you'll be transported to a patient care unit by wheelchair or gurney. Many women with morning sickness are adversely affected by motion. Be sure someone makes this fact known or the ride may be one of the worst parts of your experience.

The attendant needs to know that (1) you're ready to vomit any minute, (2) you're highly sensitive to smells and the route needs to avoid the cafeteria, as well as anyone in the elevator bringing meals to patients, (3) sudden jolts to the wheelchair or gurney will make you instantly ready to vomit; and (4) you're somewhat claustrophobic and can't tolerate crowded places.

If you find that lying on your back on a gurney watching the ceilings go by gives you motion sickness, try staring at a stationary object and breathing deeply. If you smell disagreeable odors, hold a damp facecloth over your nose. (Sprinkle it beforehand with a drop of lemon or lime juice and carry it in a Ziploc bag in your handbag.)

An antiaroma necklace can also help. Fold a large square handkerchief diagonally, three inches wide. In the center place a squeezed-out wedge of lemon or lime or a few crushed mint leaves. If other natural fragrances have greater appeal, such as pine twigs, use them. Knot the scarf loosely around the lemon or mint and place the knot of the scarf at mid-chest, about eight or nine inches below your nose. You can bring the knot closer to your nose if necessary. Have your emergency necklace packed in your handbag in a Ziploc sandwich bag. I've found that when these kits are on hand, they're less likely to be needed.

After Admission

On the patient floor, the assigned nurse will ask dozens of questions designed to help the staff take better care of patients, both physically and emotionally. Questions range from birth-control methods to food allergies. Sometimes a doctor's office makes copies of these questionnaires, which you can fill out beforehand at home. After an arduous journey from the admitting office to your patient room, you may not have the energy or interest to listen to these questions. Ask if it's okay to postpone the interview. You're well within your rights to say, "I'm not well enough to talk. I'll do it later." If the nurse seems insistent, it may be because the change of shift is coming up and these things are supposed to be done before someone else comes on.

Indicate on the questionnaire a high sensitivity to perfume and cologne—that their presence causes breathing difficulty. This is part of an effective defensive strategy. It's far easier to have a health provider put up a sign about your sensitivity to odors than to deal with visitors (and staff) individually.

Medication

Often medication is prescribed which is intended to lessen nausea and vomiting—but it doesn't always work. It's also natural to wonder whether any of these drugs may have adverse effects on your baby. In a study sponsored by the National Institutes of Health, there were fewer pregnancy losses in two groups of women who took a variety of antinausea medications than in the group who took none. Somewhat different results have been in laboratory animals, but it's unlikely that what is seen in one species of animal, given large doses of drugs over long periods will occur in humans given smaller doses over shorter time spans. Any drugs used in pregnancy come under extremely tough scrutiny from many protective agencies and universities. Your doctor is the best source of advice in each individual case.

Bendectin was a classic case. The drug was used by more than 33 million pregnant women with severe morning sickness in twenty-one countries between 1957 and 1983. It was not shown in animal trials to cause birth defects. Bendectin was finally withdrawn from the market after a number of women whose infants had birth defects sued the manufacturer and were awarded large settlements. Most obstetricians believed the drug was not responsible.

Birth defects can be caused by a variety of factors, including family genetics, use of illegal drugs as well as some prescription drugs before and during pregnancy, exposure to lead preconceptually by both the mother and the father of the child, certain viral illnesses such as measles and chicken pox, and bacterial infections. Also suspected in some cases is the advanced age of the father of the baby. In addition, exposure to toxic gases, radiation, and lead can result in damaged cells. There are some birth defects for which geneticists still have no answer. The range of reported birth defects, both major and minor, is about 2–3% overall in the general population.

Although the list of collective side effects of antinausea medications is extensive, the incidence of adverse effects is low. When any medication is required during pregnancy, doctors use the lowest dosage for the shortest period possible. If your nausea and vomiting don't abate—or even seem to get worse—during your hospital stay, your doctor needs to know. He or she will want to reexamine the type, dose, and timing of medications, the number of interruptions, the influence of roommate(s) including what they may be eating in your presence, and the generally capricious nature of nausea and vomiting.

The generic and brand names of some commonly used medications are listed below, along with some occasional side effects.

doxylamine/pyridoxine	(Bendectin: no longer given)
dimenhydrinate	(Dramamine)
diphenhydramine	(Benadryl)
meclizine	(Antivert and Bonine)
metocloramide	(Reglan)
promethazine	(Phenergan, Remsed, Mepergan)
procholorperazine	(Compazine)
thiethylperazine	(Torecan)
droperidiol	(Inapsine)

Adverse reactions to antinausea medications have been reported to include:

drowsiness	delayed gastric emptying
confusion	unsteady walking
loss of appetite	racing heart
nausea	constipation
fatigue	restlessness/insomnia
headache	possible blurred vision
altered taste	nervousness

fever
vomiting/gastrointestinal
  distress
upward rotation of the eyes
facial sweating
hallucinations
depression

bizarre dreams
irritability
chills
fine tremors
eyestrain
bronchospasm
decreased salivation

Care in the Hospital

The health-care team must try to figure out what the natural course of your case of nausea and vomiting is and minimize your physical and emotional discomfort.

Hospital care can vary, depending on the size of the institution, the experience of the staff, and the number of unusual cases treated every year. You may become a patient on a gynecological floor, a maternity/postpartum floor, a surgical unit, or a medical unit in a private room, double room, or ward. A private room is worth its weight in gold, but you must be prepared to pay extra for it in many hospitals. Ask your doctor about ordering a private room as part of your care.

If your nausea and vomiting don't respond to standard management, a frustrated doctor may request that you be visited by a psychiatrist. The old notion that vomiting in pregnancy means an unwanted pregnancy and a subconscious attempt to abort is usually the driving force behind this maneuver. But meeting with a qualified psychiatrist can be a positive experience.

If you feel negative, remember that every woman has some ambivalence about pregnancy, and it's hard to be excited about having a baby when your life has come to a grinding halt. Many women begin to question their decision to "do motherhood."

Some women suffering from severe morning sickness think about abortion, some women talk about it, and a certain percent actually terminate their pregnancies. Women who resort to abortion often do so not because the pregnancy is completely unwanted but because the physical, financial, and mental stresses have outlasted their capacity to cope.

The Empathy Factor

The sad truth is that some people have empathy and some don't. Empathy grows with exposure to a variety of situations; some people are simply theorists. If you consider how long it took the medical community to take PMS seriously, you'll understand the uphill battle women with morning sickness face.

Several ranks of medical people may be caring for you. The medical student, the junior resident, the senior resident, the fellow, the attending physician, the nurse, and the dietitian make up the team in most teaching hospitals. Some may be more empathetic than others. Each makes a contribution to care and each can solve certain problems. For example, the nurse may put off taking your vital signs at 6 A.M. to avoid an abrupt wakeup. The dietitian may be able to reassign tray delivery if you find that a certain time is best. The resident may order medications crushed and mixed into applesauce if you strongly prefer them that way.

It may be helpful to keep in mind that as advanced as medicine is, health-care workers can't necessarily "fix" everyone 100 percent. Keep in mind, too, that hospital staffs today are being pushed to "patch and dispatch"—fix patients quickly and get them out as soon as possible because of rising costs and pressure from insurance companies. With skyrocketing costs and insurance companies and medical plans requiring clients to pay a portion of the hospital bill, many people try to put off coming in for hospital care. This means today's hospitalized patients are more acutely ill than ever before, and often require more tests and procedures during their stay. That means more time—and, in teaching hospitals, more required educational instruction—which leaves less room for general TLC.

Diet

At some point in your hospital stay, a diet order will be written. It's best to work directly with the registered dietitian; ask for a consultation at the first opportunity. Depending on the hospital staffing and insurance, there may be a charge for this consultation.

Discuss with the dietitian your food successes and failures. Ask what foods and beverages are available which are not listed on the menu. As you've probably discovered, planning ahead for your next day's meals and snacks is just about impossible.

Unfortunately, most hospitals are not set up like hotels. Requests for meal replacements and food changes can't be met instantly. Ordering several extra food items on each tray, labeling them, and keeping them in the closest refrigerator may be necessary. If a food doesn't require refrigeration, keeping it on your bedside table allows a faster snack than going to a refrigerator, which may be down the hall. If you worry that the way the hospital's refrigerator smells or looks may escalate your nausea, ask your nurse to bring you the food. Many of the women I've worked with prefer to see smaller trays with less food on them and to have snacks delivered between regular meals.

Ask if there's a way to call and get your requests changed if what you ordered doesn't seem to be what your palate wants. If canned shakes—or "nutritionals," as they're called in the hospital—are available, try them. Some women say they can smell the vitamins in them; other women enjoy them tremendously. If canned nutritionals don't become favorites, ask the dietitian to send cola or lemonade. (The little bit of caffeine in a cola beverage, or an occasional cup of coffee, shouldn't cause any problems.)

Dietitians know it's difficult, if not impossible, to talk about balanced nutrition when you're feeling sick. Women who are nauseated and vomiting report great stress because they can't "eat properly." Eating a variety of foods from the recommended food groups is beyond their control, no matter how much nurses, doctors, and concerned family members and friends nudge. If the woman with morning sickness could eat better, she would. My rule is: leave her alone until she is ready to eat . . . then honor all her requests.

Most of the time, hospitals allow families to bring in requested food from home. If your food and beverage consumption is variable, sometimes the doctor or dietitian starts a "calorie count," adding up everything you eat. But a calorie count may not take into account the calories lost if you vomit. Most women agree that asking about vomit is unpleasant. Saving it for the nurse to measure is even more revolting, although commonly done.

Another drawback of a calorie count is that it's a measure of the previous day's intake, which is ancient history. Continually being told you're behind in your nutrients and calories can generate a fair degree of stress. Some women start to "power eat," trying to consume more than is comfortable because they feel as if they're being scolded for misbehaving or for failing to cooperate. The result can be more vomiting, which leads to more stress and creates what feels like a downward spiral. Try not to let a calorie count add any more stress to your situation—it's simply a tool for the dietitian to use to spot trends.

If you're to improve your success rate with meals and snacks, you need to talk with the dietitian, understanding that she or he must address any specific doctor's order. If the doctor has ordered "nutrition consult, diet per patient's tolerance," you'll have an easier time negotiating about food. However, if the doctor was trained with the tea, toast, and ginger ale crowd, it's going to be a little harder to get a cheese pizza if that's your craving of the hour. Some physicians want what they've ordered, and others let an experienced dietitian take charge.

Not every health-care provider has had extensive experience with or training in morning sickness, yours may be learning while doing. Renewed vomiting may or may not be related to a particular food you've been encouraged to eat. Just try to be patient.

Take a look at the material in Chapter 11 and remember that the people caring for you may be going by the book. If all the books say the same thing and the nurse or nutritionist follows their advice and the patient doesn't get better, it sometimes seems that the one who gets the blame is the patient. Remember, books can be wrong! Try to discuss this with your doctor or your other health-care providers.

In earlier years, getting fluids or liquids into a woman to maintain a particular level of hydration and electrolytes was critical to survival. Nowadays, with IV fluids as a backup, doctors can start you with solid foods. For some women, solids first and liquids later is far more successful in reducing the level of nausea and vomiting. Liquids can be added slowly to your routine once you've achieved gastrointestinal stability, or on your request. Keeping solids and liquids separate has been suggested by some books, but it's not an absolute rule. Whatever combination of solid and liquid food works for you should be used, whenever it works.

Supplemental Feeding

On occasion there is talk of tube feeding, especially if your food consumption stays below your needs for days at a time. Although not the answer for every woman, a tube feeding does provide nutrients, calories, and fluids. A thin tube is inserted through the nose, down the back of the throat and into the stomach. A tube feeding can give you a bit of a "claustrophobic" feeling at first. Some doctors allow you to try to eat with a tube feeding, while others prefer to wait a day or two.

If the hospital has a specialized service called nutrition support it may be possible to get special nutrients ("peripheral hyperalimentation") added to intravenous fluids for a short while, with or without the tube-feeding routine. But the IV line that goes into an arm can't deliver two thousand calories a day—the arm veins can't take the volume of fluid needed.

When it is impossible to feed "real food" or use a tube, central hyperalimentation may be considered. Central hyperalimentation uses the subclavian vein, which is next to the collarbone, rather than a vein in the arm, and completely bypasses the gastrointestinal system. The implementation of central hyperalimentation requires a trip to the operating room, and since the procedure carries a small chance of infection, it is the last resort.

"Invisible Factors"

Remember that when you're hospitalized many factors affect you that weren't present at home.

However you are being fed, it's critical that you analyze the "invisible" factors—smells, noise levels, the quality of your rest, and the number of times your sleep is interrupted. In addition, analyze the amount of motion you're subjected to. It may be anticipated or unexpected (like someone bumping into your bed), or visually experienced motion (like TV flash shots). Also consider the amount of stress and pressure you're undergoing, the level of hopefulness and optimism you can sustain under less than optimal conditions, and the amount of family and professional support you see and feel.

The chart on page 110 can help you organize this information. By plotting, you can often identify a particular set or sequence of events which disturbs your equilibrium. With that information in hand, preventive strategies can be considered.

If you're in a ward, your ability to fix things that bother you may be limited. The amount of change you can effect depends on your diplomacy and assertiveness. If you believe that the overall state of your health is declining instead of improving and the "invisible" factors can't be controlled to your satisfaction, consider going home with hydration from a home care company, if there is one in your area.

Experimental Treatments

Some researchers have cited success with the use of hypnosis or imagery techniques. It's unclear from the literature whether some of the major variables (a roommate, noise, or other natural disturbances) were removed from the scene or not. Such therapy may be more helpful in a hospital setting; you don't have to get yourself to a therapist's office. After discharge, you'd need to weigh the expense of such treatments. A less costly avenue could be to learn relaxation therapy with a licensed social worker, or you might use the money for additional baby-sitting or housework help to reduce stress.

On occasion, the use of acupuncture is tried.

Since little new research on morning sickness has been conducted and few recent successful case histories have been documented in the medical literature, practical information on bedside management is at a premium. If you've had a hospital stay and the experience has been helpful, a personal note sent to the hospital president can accomplish a great deal. First, it recognizes the efforts of your care providers. Second, it will bring attention to the misery women experience from morning sickness. Third, if you write down in detail both the most successful parts of your care and the places where improvements can be made, it will help the next woman who is admitted with morning sickness.

You might also consider making yourself available by phone to other women who must be hospitalized for morning sickness.

Sharing your experience can bring much comfort—and can even speed advances in this area of health care.

Tips for Coping with Hospitalization

You may be dreading this ultimate catastrophe, being hospitalized, but women whom I've interviewed have told me they were relieved when they were admitted, especially if they'd had a few long visits to the local emergency room for intravenous fluids. And there are a number of things you can do to make your stay more comfortable.

Ask your doctor if being admitted straight from his or her office will be faster. Sometimes women are processed through the labor and delivery suites, the usual admitting office, or the emergency room. Each route has its snags and delays. Opt for the quickest and most dignified route. Tell your doctor ahead of time that this is important for you. Ask for a private room. Even if you think you can't afford it, imagine not being able to rest well because your roommate is up all night watching TV or orders fish and broccoli at every meal, or is even sicker than you are. Even if you share a room with a postpartum woman, if she never experienced morning sickness she may not have much sympathy for you. She may be showing her baby off and sharing her joy with the world, which is to be expected. Your doctor may not understand your desire for privacy, but don't be bullied or intimidated.

Ask your doctor if he or she will be there to start the intravenous fluids when you arrive. If not, ask who you should expect to see and how long after you arrive it will take to get your IV started. You may not be processed faster because you asked; hospitals operate on the principle of "sickest first." But if you don't make your wishes known, nothing out of the ordinary will happen. If the intravenous fluid line is to be started by the "IV team," you may not be able to get a specific name. Find out who is the IV supervisor and when the shifts change. Minor confusion and delays at the change of shifts are unavoidable.

If staffers are reluctant to provide this information, be sure you have available the name and phone number of the president and vice-president of the hospital. Call them directly if you must. Hospital administrators want satisfied customers and often will make sure you're tended to as promptly as possible. Remember, you're a paying customer! Hospitals also have patient representatives. Call the main switchboard operator ahead of time for these phone numbers.

The IV nurse or technician is an important person. Because these staff members float from crisis to crisis, from floor to floor, they're not usually thanked regularly. I suggest that you ask your IV person for his or her name and then send a note of appreciation to the hospital president. You might also have a family member stash a few small boxes of fine chocolates in your tote bag as thank-you gifts to dispense during your stay. Chocolates are optional, but thank-you notes are vital.

Keeping a diary or log of your hospital experience may give you some sense of control. Ask how fast your intravenous solutions are running and when you should expect a new bag of fluid, and make a note of this information. You might ask how to tell if something is going wrong. Does your IV site hurt? Ask who will fix it and when. If you're getting medication, ask about and note the side effects. Patient care units are required to have PDR's—*Physicians' Desk Reference to Pharmaceutical Specialties and Biologicals,* which describes most medications given in hospitals—or an equivalent text. There are also hospital drug information hotlines.

Every hospital has a chief of service. If you find yourself without adequate answers, phone the chief of pharmacy directly. Keep in mind, however, that every medication has a purpose. Sometimes the medication given brings temporary relief, and sometimes the medication is meant to break a cycle. In a few cases, adverse effects may occur. No one can predict what will be the case for any given individual.

Other health-care professionals to arrange meetings with during your hospital stay are the maternity nutritionist or registered dietitian, as well as the childbirth educator, if you're planning to take prepared childbirth classes.

If you want your husband to dine with you in your hospital room, ask to meet with the director of food services to find out how to arrange it. Be ready to pay up front with a check and get the details on how things work. (Keep in mind, however, that what your husband orders may not be something you'd like to see or smell if you're feeling off.)

The more you bring to the hospital, the more you lug home.

You'll want your address book. Hospitals provide "johnnies," the short back-wrap gowns, but you may feel better if you bring your own nightclothes—like a bright knee-length, short-sleeved nightgown and baggy bloomer underpants. Most hospitals provide toothbrush, toothpaste, and soap kits, as well as shapeless green foam nonskid slippers. Don't bring any valuables, and mark your clothes ahead of time with an indelible marker. You may be cold because you're dehydrated; a shawl is probably a good idea, since it's loose and easy to put on and take off.

I recommend bringing two clean bras; four pairs of underpants; a hip bag with your medical cards, driver's license, one or two checks, lipstick, blush, address book, and $10 or less (for newspapers and possibly gum from the gift shop); three pairs of white athletic socks; slippers; a colorful nightgown; a shawl; hard candies; your own water if you've found a variety you prefer; three boxes of assorted crackers (most hospitals only provide soda crackers); and a small plastic pail with a lid if possible (you may be sick away from your room, and while hospitals provide "emesis" basins, these are generally small kidney-shaped plastic containers without lids which can be difficult to hold). Some women bring swimmers' nose clips to block disagreeable smells when they're trying to sleep. Earplugs might come in handy, since hospitals sometimes aren't as quiet as you might think. Sometimes hospitals buy budget-quality facial tissue, which can be rough or carry a particular scent. You might bring your own.

It's a good idea to bring your own pillow and maybe a portable cassette recorder and a "white noise" cassette to help you sleep. Bring enlarged copies of the signs in this book to put on your door when you arrive. Bring a small roll of tape, too.

You may want to bring a pocket-sized calorie content booklet to help keep track of your caloric intake, or refer to page 100.

Most hospitals have lending libraries, but you might consider getting a book or two out of your local library from the "large type" area.

Family and friends may send flowers. Some hospitals provide vases, but many don't. Consider bringing a mayonnaise jar. By the time you leave the hospital, most cut flowers will have lost their charm and you won't want to drag them home with you. You'll hardly miss the mayonnaise jar, either. Some flowers are refreshing, while others are overpowering. If possible, ask for favors (errands, for example) instead of flowers.

Bring a small box of blank notecards stamped and with your home address, and write your hospital thank-you (or improvement) notes daily so you don't forget.

When you're picked up at discharge, be sure to have someone evaluate how many cars are usually running in the area. Some hospitals have covered drive-up areas to protect patients from inclement weather. The downside of this is that car exhaust fumes are also trapped underneath, which can be extremely nauseating. If your husband (or whoever comes to fetch you) has to park in a nonregulation zone, be sure he puts a sign in the window saying "Emergency: transporting pregnant woman." Some hospitals offer valet parking; be sure the valet doesn't smoke in your car! Most pickup traffic is scheduled for midmorning, and it may be helpful to pick an off hour to leave.

Some insurance companies require that the patient call in daily to get "an okay." Be sure to write down the first and last names of the people you talk with and exactly what they tell you to do. If you're asked for a doctor's letter, get it that day. Before you mail it, be sure you have a copy for your files.

If you chose to read your chart, and you have every right to do so, a hospital staffer will be assigned to help you understand the terminology.

Remember, hospitals can be intimidating when you don't feel well, but they needn't be considered untameable monsters. You have the right to ask questions about options, and you also have the right to decline any particular treatment if you think it's not helpful. If you decide to leave the hospital before your doctor discharges you, or "AMA" (against medical advice), your insurance company may not pay for the visit. This scenario is rare, as generally insurance companies can't get their patients out the door fast enough. Some insurance companies will pay for home hydration therapy and some won't. Find out ahead of time what sort of coverage you have, as it may make a difference in your discharge care.

Quick Nutrient Calculator

Item	Amount	Calories	Protein (in grams)
Liquids			
Club soda	12 oz	0	0
Tonic water	12 oz	120	0
Ginger ale	12 oz	115	0
Cola	12 oz	140	0
Milk, skim	8 oz	80	8
Milk, low-fat	8 oz	100	8
Milk, whole	8 oz	150	8
Apple juice	4 oz	60	0
Lemonade	8 oz	70	0
Cocoa	8 oz	220	9
Starches			
Cream of wheat	4 oz	70	2
Cold cereal	½ cup	75(avg)	2
Toast	1 slice	75	2
Rice cake	1 (3 in.)	50	1
English muffin	1 whole	150	4
Corn muffin	1 small	145	3
Mashed potatoes	½ cup	75	2
Noodles	½ cup	100	2
Rice	½ cup	100	3
French fries	1 oz	150	2
Popcorn	1 oz	140	2
Pretzels	1 oz	95	2
Pancakes, 2	3-in. dia.	120	4
Saltines	6	70	2

Quick Nutrient Calculator (Continued)

Item	Amount	Calories	Protein (in grams)
Vegetables			
Squash	½ cup	40	1
Creamed corn	½ cup	80	2
Green beans	½ cup	30	1
Carrots, raw	½ cup	25	1
Tomato	1 whole	30	1
Broccoli	½ cup	30	1
Mixed salad	2 cups	50	1
Desserts			
Tapioca	½ cup	110	4
Custard	½ cup	150	7
Ice cream	½ cup	150	3
Gelatin	½ cup	80	1
Popsicle	3 oz	70	0
Sherbet	½ cup	120	3
Angel-food cake	1/12th	90	2
Soups and Entrees			
Chicken rice soup	½ cup	30	2
Grilled cheese sandwich	1	325	18
Macaroni and cheese	6 oz	200	11
Chicken pot pie	8 oz	450	15
Pizza, cheese	4 oz	320	14
Skinless chicken breast	2 oz	160	14

C H A P T E R 11

Your Survival Kit

By now, you probably have a fairly good perspective on the variable nature of morning sickness. Nevertheless, if you're suffering from nausea or vomiting, getting through *today* requires significant emotional fortitude. If your case is severe, the promise of improved overall stability is a critical aspect. But that promise may seem out of reach.

Many women reluctantly admit that it's difficult to think about continuing a pregnancy when doing so means disability and misery, suffered alone. Society's attitude—reflected in remarks like "Oh, it's nothing to worry about" and "Be glad you're pregnant" —has a lot to do with a woman's ability to cope.

As discussed in the previous chapter, even hospital care doesn't necessarily bring a "cure" and can carry its own special disruptions and ignominies.

This chapter is a package of hints and encouragements to help you get through your morning sickness.

Warning Signs

It's often easier to relay information about your condition to others in advance than to attempt it at the beginning of a crisis. To that end, I've created a few signs for you to post near your hospital bed, at home, in the office, or wherever you're staying.

Most women I've worked with have said that when they feel the worst it's easiest just to say, "I'm doing what the doctor/dietitian/ books say to do." The following signs can be copied, perhaps even enlarged, using a copy machine, or clipped out of the book. In fact, you might want to have a copy of the book where family, friends or coworkers can pick it up and learn more about what you're going through.

Danger/Danger/Danger
Danger/Danger
Sensitive Nose Ahead!
Unstable Stomach Condition
VOMITING COULD OCCUR
Smell Watch/ Smell Watch/ Smell Watch

For the Office

WARNING/WARNING/WARNING
WARNING/WARNING

Right now my sense of smell is extremely sensitive so I'd appreciate if you WOULDN'T

1. Sit too close to me.
2. Bring your coffee cup within twenty feet of my desk.
3. Breathe on me.
4. Wear too much cologne, perfume, or aftershave.
5. Use any cleaning agents or sprays or bring wash pails close to my area.
6. Leave the coffeepot on all day.
7. Smoke close to me.
8. _____
9. _____

Both my baby and I thank you for your compassion and sensitivity.

For the Household and Any Guests

WARNING:
FRAGILE HOSTESS AHEAD

1. Welcome to this humble home.
2. Please acquaint yourself with the kitchen, dishes, stove, refrigerator, and sink.
3. Presently I am suffering from an ancient ailment: Motherhood Miseries, a.k.a. Morning Sickness, a.k.a. Hyperemesis Gravidarum.
4. Primary symptom: Radar Nose. I smell everything.
5. Please wash your own dishes, clean up after yourself, and do not use perfume, cologne, aftershave, or hairspray in this house.
6. Please don't smoke in my house or in my car.
7. To get brownie points (circle what applies), you can offer to change my other child's diapers, take the trash out, feed the cat, and change the litter box.

(fill in further requests)_____

_____

Both my baby and I appreciate your understanding and help in reducing the factors which add to the uncontrollable problems of nausea (and vomiting).

Tracking the Good and Bad Times

As I mentioned earlier, you need to note the invisible factors which can have a major impact on your well-being. A tracking sheet is provided on page 110. Before recording any information, make several copies of the blank sheets for future use.

The tracking sheet is basically a journal of your progress. There are several variables which most women consider negative, all involving the senses; these appear at the top of the page.

The times at which you take medication, eat, or drink can make a big difference. The duration of any average activity can be a make-or-break factor. Once you're aware that everything affects your gastric stability and plot all the variables, a pattern generally emerges. A rating scale of 1 (worst) to 10 (best) can help pinpoint positive and negative factors.

Record any and all variables, since that's the only way to analyze both the invisible trigger and stabilizer factors. Various foods and beverages will probably have a predictable pattern of appeal once you've compiled the rest of the data.

You may note that the presence or absence of humidity in the morning can set the tone for the day. One woman discovered that when humidity was high in the morning her day's activity was minimal. However, when the morning was much less humid her activity increased dramatically by early afternoon. But overactivity in the afternoon resulted in a crash by early evening, a crash which lasted for the next two or two and a half days. Once this trend was spotted and discussed, she tapered her activities on low-humidity days and prevented recurrence.

(Keeping a food diary can be extremely helpful, too. Recipes considered as well as those used or modified should be noted. This may help you or others zero in on future food possibilities.)

For example, on Susie's tracking sheet she notes that husband Fred's tossing and turning resulted in his facing and breathing on her as soon as she woke up. This set off her morning sickness, which she rated "1," or really bad. She found that after vomiting she regained some of her composure by sitting in the cool morning air on the back porch; she rated this "3." She wanted something cold, textured, and bland to settle her stomach and found relief with a rice cake and a small amount of ice chips (made from distilled water and stored in the freezer in a sealed Ziploc bag). She felt a bit weak and continued to rate her condition "3."

Susie was just beginning to feel as if she could dress when Fred decided to turn on the news. The sudden loud sound made her jump and become tense, maintaining her "3" status. Susie yelled at Fred to turn down the volume and decided to keep sitting on the porch for another twenty minutes. She blew Fred a kiss through the screen door and asked him not to hug her, since he'd put on aftershave. She ate a few more ice chips and decided to go inside and dress. Fred had put canned food out for the dog, Mugzie, and after one step into the house, Susie retreated to the

Time	Score 1–10	Level of Smells	Amount of Motion	Any Noise	Pref. Taste	Texture of Food Eaten	Quality of Climate	Time
6 A.M.	wake up—1—Fred breathed on me							
7 A.M.	3 sat on porch—clean air. Bland rice cake. (want dry textured food)							
8 A.M.	3 no noise! Fred turned on the news loudly!							
9 A.M.	4 dog food! (in kitchen) to porch again.							
10 A.M.	5 feel better. Tent dress. Drove to work.							
11 A.M.	6 sat in office—Door closed. Ate ham and cheese sand.							
12 NOON	3! Old coffee pot & muggy stale air in Boss's office							
1 P.M.	5 (want crunch & sweet) Ate fresh orange & raw carrots.							
2 P.M.	7 (want cold & sweet) craving ice cream—frozen yogurt OK but not quite "it"							
3 P.M.	7→6 getting tired—better leave early!							
4 P.M.	5 pooped. opened refrigerator at home! Smell of old food→							
5 P.M.	8 feel better. Called Fred to get "to go" food and eat outside on porch.							

porch for more fresh air and hopes of maintaining a slightly improved rating of "4." She ate a few more ice chips.

An hour later, at "5," Susie had a shower, dressed uneventfully, and drove to work with a prepacked lunch bag which contained an "air sickness" bag, a clean, wet facecloth, and fresh lemon. The stop-and-go motion in the parking garage, and the closed-up feeling, caused low-level queasiness, which Susie was able to ward off by smelling the lemon. When she parked her car, she took a drink of the cold seltzer she carried in her cooler. She noted her gastrointestinal status as "6."

Susie arrived at her desk after coffee break and before lunch so that food smells were at a low level. She promptly ate a ham and cheese sandwich, and at lunchtime headed out to walk to avoid

Time	Meds Taken	Activity	Place	Duration N/V	Amt. Fluids
6 A.M.	– (no meds.) ran to bathroom			15 min.	none
7 A.M.	slow moving			no n/v	½ c ice chips
8 A.M.	Air crisp cool. on porch.			no n/v.	½ c. ice chips
9 A.M.	Lied down a recliner. Cold pack to neck.			no v little n	½ c. ice
10 A.M.	no traffic. Little queasy. Smelled the lemon				½ c. seltzer
11 A.M.	Walked at lunch. Used sunglasses			–n!	1 c. "Brown cow"
12 NOON	→ bathroom			+v	2 c. ice → felt better
1 P.M.	Liz (perfume!) → spoke from door way			–n.	2 c. ice water
2 P.M.	feel hot—take off shoes → OK				1 c. cold gingerale
3 P.M.	open car windows until saw city bus → closed quick!				
4 P.M.	↑ nausea			↑v → took 1 hr nap	
5 P.M.	took my (non pregnant) vitamin pill ate grilled cheese & tomato (bland & tart) sandwich. ½ c. milk → feel OK.				

cafeteria food smells. She'd made progress: she now rated her condition "6." Since the sun was bright, she wore sunglasses and walked with her friend Millie, who respected her need for peace and quiet. The ham and cheese sandwich and the walk made Susie thirsty, so she made herself a "brown cow" (half cola and half low-fat milk) at the snack bar in the cafeteria. She was free of nausea, a "6," until she was on her way back to her office desk, when she felt instantly queasy. Looking around, she spied a filmy coffeepot with one inch of well-cooked coffee. Her status plummeted to "3." She ran to the bathroom, losing part of her lunch. She then sat with a cold facecloth on her forehead while crunching on ice chips.

About an hour later Susie had recovered to about a "5" and

wanted something crunchy and sweet, which she decided would be a fresh orange and carrot sticks. Her old office-mate Liz stopped by for a chat, but Liz's newest perfume made Susie bolt out of her chair and down the hall for fresh air. When she felt better, she said as diplomatically as possible, "Liz, no offense to you but your perfume and my stomach just aren't going to be buddies." Two cups of ice-cold water with a twist of lime, sipped slowly, went down well, boosting her fluid total for the day so far to 5¼ cups, or slightly over half of the "stay-even" allowance set by her prenatal nutritionist.

At two o'clock Susie's taste buds asked for vanilla ice cream, with a rating of "7." She was marginally satisfied after having to settle for vanilla frozen yogurt. The office had warmed up now that the sun was pouring through the window, and Susie felt the need to shed her shoes and plant her feet on the bare wooden floor. The sweetness of the yogurt made her thirsty, and she decided a cold can of ginger ale from the vending machine might be called for. Twelve ounces later she continued to feel well, or at "7."

By three o'clock Susie felt a decline setting in and decided to leave early to avoid a "crash" in the office. She drove with the car windows open until she was passed by a Greyhound bus, when she hurriedly closed the windows. Twenty minutes later she turned into the driveway of her new ranch house. Opening the refrigerator door proved to be a mistake; the smell of Fred's leftover take-out dinner leaped out and instantly provoked nausea and a dry retch or two. An hour's nap saved the afternoon. By 5 P.M. Susie had called Fred's office, suggesting he bring home another take-out dinner for two and they would dine on the back porch while the sun set. Fred arrived home with dinner for two, picked up at the local deli, and found Susie munching on a grilled cheese and tomato sandwich Mrs. Jones next door had delivered. Susie hadn't been able to wait. Fred smiled and shrugged.

As you can see from Susie's chart, there were numerous variables which needed to be identified quickly. Both negative and positive factors differed in their impact. Only by regularly listing key events will you be able to take defensive action. Listen to the messages you're hearing from your body.

Activities

Being homebound can generate both boredom and restlessness. The nausea decreases your attention span, yet distractions and activities remain necessary. Your chosen tasks should require a fair amount of concentration but probably not much thinking. Learning something new requires a fair amount of mental energy. If the activity is too grand in scope, it may generate mental fatigue and stress. Here are a few activities which do not require large dollar investments or tremendous mental labors:

Making beaded barrettes or belts with a kit.

Watching an ant farm and reading a children's book on what goes on in it.

Watching birds at a feeder attached to the bedroom window, using inexpensive binoculars and a bird book.

Writing a child's storybook for the baby's third or fourth birthday, complete with pictures.

Stargazing with a telescope and star chart.

Turning doodles into greeting cards.

Listening to books on tape. (Check your local library before going to the bookstore.)

Reading short stories onto tapes to give to sight-impaired booklovers.

Reading children's stories onto tapes for Christmas, birthday, or sick-day presents. (These could be helpful for your own baby-sitters in later years.)

Planting flowers in a window box and watching them grow.

Caring for goldfish or exotic fish.

Origami

Watching educational videos.

Rewriting your address book.

Playing with Lego or Tinker Toys.

Playing Scrabble or other word games.

Organizing a photo album.

Swapping activity lists with other women in your situation.

Eating a fortune cookie a day and saving the fortunes.

Clipping and saving your horoscope from the daily newspaper.

Time	Score (1–10)	Level of Smells	Amount of Motion	Any Noise	Preference Taste	Texture of Food Eaten	Quality of Climate
6 A.M.							
7 A.M.							
8 A.M.							
9 A.M.							
10 A.M.							
11 A.M.							
Noon							
1 P.M.							
2 P.M.							
3 P.M.							
4 P.M.							
5 P.M.							
6 P.M.							
7 P.M.							
8 P.M.							
9 P.M.							
10 P.M.							
11 P.M.							
Midnight							
1 A.M.							
2–4 A.M.							
5 A.M.							

Time	Medication Taken	Activity	Place	Duration N/V	Amount Fluids
6 A.M.					
7 A.M.					
8 A.M.					
9 A.M.					
10 A.M.					
11 A.M.					
Noon					
1 P.M.					
2 P.M.					
3 P.M.					
4 P.M.					
5 P.M.					
6 P.M.					
7 P.M.					
8 P.M.					
9 P.M.					
10 P.M.					
11 P.M.					
Midnight					
1 A.M.					
2 A.M.					
3 A.M.					
4–6 A.M.					

Pressing any get-well flowers to frame later.

Reading a great book, like *A Natural History of the Senses* by Diane Ackerman. If nothing else, the descriptions will generate laughter.

Listening to relaxation tapes.

Making old-fashioned paper dolls and doll clothes for a local fund drive, such as the Salvation Army Christmas drive.

Rereading the books you loved as a child.

Knitting or embroidering.

Starting a small herb garden using pots on a sunny windowsill. Choose some that smell good to you.

CHAPTER 12

The Importance of D.I.E.T.: Post-Crisis and for the Rest of Your Life

Once the nausea and vomiting have passed, it's time to try to eat nutritious foods again. If you're to stay healthy, you need to D.I.E.T. —which stands for "Developing Intelligent Eating Techniques."

Schedule an appointment with a registered dietitian (R.D.) for a complete nutritional assessment. A registered dietitian will evaluate the nutrient contribution of the foods you usually eat. Certain foods may remain problematic for you. If you can't tolerate milk, for example, your diet may be low in calcium, as well as vitamin B2, riboflavin. The R.D. will help find alternative ways to provide any missing nutrients to your diet and will discuss with you better ways to prepare food.

Only after a careful analysis of your usual intake will the R.D. suggest supplemental vitamins and minerals. One reason for this is that some nutrients (calcium, for example) are better absorbed from foodstuffs than from pills. Some supplemental minerals, like iron, may be constipating, whereas iron found in prune juice is not. Delicate relationships exist among the various nutrients, and they are easily disturbed if the dose of any supplement is excessive —or over 100 percent of the recommended dietary allowance (RDA). A carefully selected daily diet can supply many of the nutrients needed for a healthy pregnancy.

Try to eat according to this general daily-minimum guide:

4 servings from the dairy group
9 or more servings from the fruit and vegetable groups

11 or more servings from the grains/breads groups
2 (3-ounce) servings from the protein/meat group
3 to 4 teaspoons fat

When you begin to feel well again after morning sickness, it's advisable to add gradually to your diet. Your body must readapt to food, trying too hard and too fast to regain lost weight can cause problems.

No one food contains all the nutrients you need when you're pregnant, so variety is the word. Check out the list of nutrients which fall into each food grouping below and the need for a sensible balance will become obvious.

THE MEAT/PROTEIN GROUP

Fish
Poultry
Beef
Pork
Lamb
Eggs
Low-fat cheeses
Legumes (with rice)
Tofu

The calories, or energy, provided by these foods come from complete protein and, in many cases, from hidden fat. Meats should be lean, with fat trimmed off.

Foods in this group contain the following vitamins and minerals:

Thiamin (vitamin B1)
Riboflavin (vitamin B2)
Niacin
Vitamin B6
Vitamin A
Vitamin D
Vitamin K
Calcium
Chloride

Cobalt
Phosphorus
Sodium
Zinc
Copper
Iodine
Iron
Biotin
Pantothenic acid
Folic acid (or folate)
Vitamin B12
Molybdenum
Potassium
Magnesium
Sulfur

THE DAIRY GROUP

Low-fat and skim milk
Low-fat yogurt
Low-fat cottage cheese
Ice milk
Low-fat cheeses

Calories, or energy, in this group come from complete protein, some fat, and some carbohydrate.

The following vitamins and minerals are found in dairy foods:

Thiamin (vitamin B1)
Riboflavin (vitamin B2)
Vitamin A
Vitamin D
Calcium
Chloride
Phosphorus
Sodium
Sulfur
Magnesium
Biotin
Vitamin B12

Potassium
Zinc
Selenium

THE FRUIT AND VEGETABLE GROUP

Fruits/Juices

Apple
Apple juice
Orange*
Orange juice*
Cranberry juice
Banana*
Pear
Peach*
Pineapple*
Prunes*
Prune juice
Kiwi*
Mango*
Guava*
Strawberries*
Blueberries*
Raspberries*
Blackberries*
Cherries*
Grapes*
Plums*
Apricots*
Apricot nectar*

Vegetables

Asparagus
Broccoli*
Brussels sprouts*
Cabbage, red and green*

*High nutrient value.

Dandelion greens*
Endive
Cauliflower
Carrots
Eggplant
Kale*
Mustard greens*
Parsnips
Green and yellow beans
Yams*
Sweet potatoes*
Peas
Potatoes*
Tomatoes*
Zucchini
Winter squash*
Pumpkins

Fruit and vegetable group calories, or energy, come from simple and complex carbohydrates. These foods contain the following vitamins and minerals:

Riboflavin (vitamin B2)
Niacin
Vitamin A
Vitamin E
Vitamin K
Calcium
Phosphorus
Potassium
Copper
Iron
Magnesium
Molybdenum
Folic acid
Ascorbic acid
Fiber
Manganese

THE BREADS/CEREALS/STARCHY VEGETABLES GROUP

Rice
Pasta
Noodles
Potatoes
Corn
Peas
Squash (winter type)
Wheat, rye, oatmeal, white bread
Crackers
Rolls
Whole grain-cooked cereal
Ready-to-eat dry cereal
Popcorn (unbuttered)
Muffins
Tabbouleh (made from cracked bulgur wheat)

Bread/cereal group calories, or energy, come from complex carbohydrates and incomplete protein. They provide the following vitamins and minerals:

Thiamin (vitamin B2)
Niacin
Vitamin B6
Selenium
Phosphorus
Sulfur
Zinc
Copper
Iron
Magnesium
Manganese
Molybdenum
Pantothenic acid
Biotin
Potassium
Fiber

Chromium
Selenium

Current nutrition research suggests that the amount of fat in the overall daily diet should be kept at 30 percent of total calories. There are three general types of fats to consider: polyunsaturated, monounsaturated, and saturated.

The amount of saturated fat in food seems to be correlated most strongly with major disease, which is why nutritionists suggest eating less than 10 percent of your total daily calories from this type. Saturated fats are generally solid at room temperature and are found in meats, cheeses, and milk products, in addition to palm-kernel and coconut oils. Monounsaturated oils include olive and canola. Polyunsaturated oils include corn, safflower, and sunflower. Again, nutritionists recommend you get about 10 percent of your total daily calories from these last two types as well. Some foods have fats built in—like cookies, crackers, pastries, and prepared foods.

Here's a quick review of what each of the nutrients listed in the RDA's does. This is a streamlined version. For more details, consult a book on nutrition or see a registered dietitian.

Protein: helps to keep muscles intact, builds red blood cells, makes antibodies (germ fighters), maintains the structural parts of the body.

Carbohydrates: provide the body with quick energy. Many nutrients are found in carbohydrate foods.

Fats: provide three essential fatty acids, which keep the skin looking healthy. Getting enough is not generally a problem.

Vitamin A: keeps eyes healthy.

Vitamin C: keeps intact the connective tissue (the tissue that holds your blood vessels together as well as holding bones to muscles), reduces bruising, keeps gums strong.

Vitamin D: with phosphorus and calcium, keeps bones and teeth strong.

Vitamin K: helps blood clot effectively.

Vitamin E: protects cells from oxidation (a process which destroys them).

Thiamin (also known as vitamin B1): functions to release energy from carbohydrate foods. Also aids in proper functioning of the heart, gastrointestinal tract, and nervous system.

Riboflavin (also known as vitamin B2): functions to release energy from carbohydrates, proteins, and fats, and to make red blood cells.

Niacin: functions to release energy from carbohydrates; also contributes to fat synthesis and metabolism.

Vitamin B6: important in the metabolism of carbohydrates, fats, and protein; proper functioning of the central nervous system; and other activities.

Vitamin B12: important for the normal functioning of the gastrointestinal tract, bone marrow (red blood cell production), and nervous system, and for growth. Involved in formation of myelin, the coating around the nerves, and in the metabolism of carbohydrates, proteins, and fat. Prevents serious anemia.

Biotin: needed for many enzyme systems in the body.

Pantothenic acid: part of enzyme systems. Important for the proper metabolism of carbohydrates, proteins, and fats.

Folic acid: necessary for the production of DNA, and the functioning of two amino acids. Also essential for the formation of both white and red blood cells.

Choline: important for the proper metabolism of fats.

Calcium: important for strong bones and teeth, muscle and heart contractions, and blood clotting.

Phosphorus: works with calcium and vitamin D to make strong bones and teeth, and aids many metabolic reactions in the body.

Magnesium: for many energy reactions, proper blood clotting, and muscular contractions.

Iron: carries oxygen to all cells in the body, and is part of many enzyme systems.

Zinc: part of many enzyme systems in the body.

Iodine: part of the thyroid hormones, which regulate the body's metabolism.

Selenium: functions to protect other nutrients.

Copper: important in many enzyme systems and in preventing anemia.

Manganese: important in enzyme systems, for proper reproduction, growth, and bone and cartilage function and glucose metabolism.

Fluoride: Strengthens bones and teeth.

Chromium: important for proper glucose metabolism.

Molybdenum: important in many enzyme systems.

Sodium: important in the maintenance of fluid balance in the body.

Potassium: important for nerve functioning, skeletal muscle contractions, and maintaining blood pressure.

Chloride: essential for maintaining fluid and electrolyte balance.

C H A P T E R 13

Real Stories of Real Women

Over the past few years, I have queried many women with morning sickness about their particular experiences in pregnancy. In almost all cases the women were perfectly healthy beforehand, and all had great difficulty with being sick and being referred to as sick. They told me again and again the debility that resulted from constant nausea, but said that few others were really aware of their incapacity. Smells were generally noted as the mortal enemy, capable of ruining any moment or any day.

Here are the true stories of several women, all of whom were hospitalized at some point in at least one of their pregnancies. Names and events have been altered slightly to maintain anonymity. Each of these women's situation is unique in its particular details, yet they all have much in common.

Annie

Annie had an uneventful second pregnancy, and as she told me, "I deserve it!" Two years earlier, at age twenty-two, she'd become pregnant for the first time. She lived with her husband in a town on the Rhode Island coast. Her nausea and vomiting started at the beginning of August, the second month of her pregnancy.

Also in August began her encampment in the master bedroom, near an overworked air conditioner. Living on iced tea for fluid, Annie could tolerate cold fruit salad only when she was feeling "better." That particular summer was unbearably hot and humid. The foods she chose to eat were described as "cold"; she even ate cold bread. She found it easier to breathe if the air was extremely cold. Hot, humid air made her breathless and instantly nauseated. She would wrap herself up in a winter blanket and stay in the bedroom for days on end.

Five feet, 4 inches tall, she started her pregnancy a bit over-weight at 150 pounds. In November, her fifth month, her weight was 147 pounds. By this point in her pregnancy, she should have gained 6 to 10 pounds over her prepregnancy weight; she had had a net loss of 9 to 13 pounds.

When the heat in the house was turned on for the first time in November, she reacted poorly to the smell of "roasted dust." She had not been well enough to do the usual fall cleaning, which included vacuuming the radiators. When the scorched dust smell was eliminated, her gastrointestinal equilibrium returned.

In January, at month 7, she had strong cravings for melon, grapes and pineapples, which were out of season and hard to get. She ate green peppers, tomatoes, croutons, lettuce, and carrots with Thousand Island dressing, but only early in the afternoon. Italian dressing was out. On one occasion when she craved Japanese food, her husband took her to a favorite restaurant, an event she eagerly anticipated. Once she was inside the door, waves of nausea forced her to dash outside, and she vomited on the street. Another time, her husband took her to a marvelous restaurant in a Boston skyscraper. Once seated, she was unable to eat because the restaurant was filled with "heavy fall food smells all around."

She was unable to eat beef or eggs, formerly among her favorite foods. Turkey sandwiches were benign because, as she put it, "turkey doesn't have much smell or taste anyway." The items she found predictably safe were potato chips, cold fruit, sweet "textured" cake and cookies, chocolate ice cream, strawberries, Bigelow's breakfast tea with sugar, and white toast with butter.

She commented that as her morning sickness continued past the "magic first trimester mark," her husband became more and more distant. She later discovered that he felt ill himself when she vomited. He felt entirely responsible for her morning sickness and experienced an overwhelming sense of helplessness and hopelessness. When he left the scene during her bouts of vomiting, he felt better—but guilty.

The smells which triggered Annie's nausea and vomiting included food smells, especially the gravy from Salisbury steak, and garlic bread. She said that bodily smells, especially perfume, were destabilizing factors and she knew she was smelling "smells no one else could smell." Cigarette smoke, she said, went "right to my stomach," but for some strange reason she tolerated smoke from her father-in-law's fireplace fairly well. The taste of plain water would precipitate vomiting, but drinking ice-cold unsweetened iced tea worked "just fine," so she continued to drink it to the end of her pregnancy.

In March, when she delivered a full-term, healthy baby girl, Annie's weight was 165 pounds, only 15 pounds over her beginning weight.

Betsy

Admitted three times overnight to the emergency room for hydration, Betsy was eventually admitted to a hospital GYN unit. She was pregnant for the second time. She told one of her health-care providers she had lost her first baby because of the constant nausea and vomiting. The nurse who noted this information thought it was a curious situation, since the medical literature attests to the contrary. Once she was comfortable with her care providers, Betsy described being admitted "about a dozen times" in her first pregnancy to the emergency room of a large hospital in another state, before one or two stays on a patient care unit.

Although she was seen frequently, she considered the care she received ineffective, because her relief was short-lived. She felt as if she was always "bothering someone." She added, "I thought they all looked at me like I was some sort of freak because I just never got over the nausea and vomiting like they said I would." After a while, when the staff was totally frustrated, a psychiatrist was called to visit. His comment to her was that she was "probably vomiting just to upset the nurses!"

Once she was given Tigan suppositories, an antinausea medication. When she complained of lower abdominal cramping, which started the vomiting again, an exhausted resident was called to the floor to evaluate the situation. He returned about ten minutes later with a small tube and said the only alternative was a tube feeding. Not wanting to appear uncooperative, she allowed him to attempt to insert the tube into her nose, unfortunately without the benefit of nasal xylocaine, an anesthetic. He explained that the tube needed to be pushed through her nose, and would go down her esophagus and into her stomach. After that, she'd be hooked up to a machine which dispensed a formula. The thin tube being inserted into her left nasal passage produced an uncomfortable sensation and she started to retch and cry.

Feeling panicky, Betsy tried to explain that she was about to vomit, but the warning was too late. She vomited green bile on the resident's lab coat. This ended the tube feeding effort. In the morning, the resident said, another doctor would be around to decide what other courses should be considered. Betsy finally fell asleep at 4 A.M., vowing she'd be out of the emergency room by 8 A.M. Still miserable, Betsy lied to the morning nurse and said she had heard her mother was terribly ill and she had to leave immediately.

Her current doctor had been in contact with Betsy's former care provider, and learned that she had decided to terminate her first pregnancy after eleven weeks of constant nausea and vomiting, no sleep or relief, the traumatic emergency room episode, and finally losing her job.

With the news of her second pregnancy and subsequent hospital admission, she said, "I hope it doesn't happen again." Her nurse thought she meant the morning sickness, but in fact Betsy was worrying about having enough stamina to endure what might be weeks of misery.

Having moved to a new state with her husband because of his new job, she hoped she was ready to start a family . . . again. When she learned that other women were also hospitalized with debilitating morning sickness, she was relieved. During her nutritional assessment, she spontaneously volunteered lists of smell aversions, cravings, and other strange feelings she had noticed but had discounted as idiosyncratic. She was also relieved to learn that "Radar Nose" was a common complaint.

This second pregnancy was punctuated with several emergency room admissions for hydration therapy. Betsy's husband, Joe, accompanied her on most visits. On one occasion he commented that although he'd initially wanted several children, if he got one, he'd be happy. "I can't stand to see Betsy go through this. Most of her family and many of my friends think she's making it up, but I see her retching over the toilet at night, crying. It's not a fake. There's nothing I can do to help. I feel like it's all my fault.''

One favorite food item for Betsy turned out to be the diet soda Fresca, something she'd never drunk before her illness. For a time she found raspberry ginger ale successful and ate Reese's peanut butter cups for a few days. She couldn't eat anything except pasta for more than a day or two. During the nine long months of her pregnancy, Betsy's doctor saw her more often as an emergency case for dehydration therapy than as a regular obstetrical client. He jokingly said to Betsy one night at 2 A.M., while he was inserting an intravenous line into her arm, that he thought someone had changed his office address without telling him.

As she learned to live with chronic nausea, Betsy made herself available by phone to other women newly suffering from morning sickness.

Finally the baby was born, full-term and healthy. Betsy decided to breast-feed and take advantage of all the "motherly experiences" because, as she put it, "I think I've just had my last baby. As much as we love her, I can't imagine doing this again.''

Connie

A successful woman with her own business, Connie had received hospital treatment twice previously for "the same problem." Before the official confirmation of her second pregnancy, Connie knew she was pregnant: she noted that one day while dressing her son, she became acutely aware that the baby "smelled." The smell, she said, was not unclean, just "a real strong people smell." She noticed that her laundry now smelled of heavy perfume, but she had changed neither her detergent nor her method of laundering. Clothes from the cleaners had a chemical odor.

As Connie's nausea progressed to vomiting, her weight fell ten pounds. Her doctor decided hospitalization was necessary the day she collapsed in her office. What she did not tell her doctor was that the previous week she had flown for two hours to an important business meeting. The plane hit about twenty minutes of very turbulent air, which rendered Connie hopelessly sick in a first-class lavatory. She had purposely bought an expensive first-class seat to avoid food smells from other travelers, but hadn't banked on a bad flight. She was so weak at the end of the trip that the stewardess insisted she be transported in a wheelchair. Needless to say, she canceled her meeting.

During her hospital stay, Connie had a greenish complexion (jaundice), which seemed to get worse as the days went on and she was unable to eat or drink. To keep her mind off her misery, she conducted business over the phone. This diversionary activity caused an older nurse to conclude that "she is in here because she only wants a vacation from taking care of her child! How can she be sick if she can work? Does she look sick to you?"

Like Betsy, Connie found comfort in the "Radar Nose" hypothesis. "Who really cares if it hasn't been scientifically validated? Just look at that old theory about double estrogens being the cause of morning sickness. I was hospitalized many more times with my first pregnancy, lost far more weight, and was my doctor surprised when I had a boy!"

Connie was discharged after a seven-day hospital stay, but she still made numerous trips to the emergency room for intravenous fluids. She'd once had an adverse reaction to an antinausea medication, so her doctor was reluctant to use another. Smell management became paramount. Connie noted that in the late afternoon, about four-thirty, she needed to rest in a dark bedroom or she would become violently sick. The slightest fatigue started the downhill spiral. She was occasionally able to return to her office to work for an hour or two. She commented that if she worked for someone else, "they'd probably have fired me long ago."

Visiting Connie after her baby was born, all the family members displayed absolute enthusiasm and merriment. However, one aunt commented that she wished information about morning sickness had been around when she was pregnant, thirty years before. As she put it, "I suffered so much, it was like a living hell."

Dagmar

When Dagmar and her husband were considering a third child, she phoned me to ask what was new in the way of morning sickness management. Three years earlier I had met this attractive, slight, pale woman in the hospital when she was pregnant for the second time and being fed through a line in her neck. Dagmar's medical record indicated that she had also required hospitalization with her first pregnancy, though not as extensively.

When we tried to understand the triggers which affected Dagmar at home, heightened senses emerged as a major theme. Through many interviews, Dagmar provided clues to a management approach which focused on exploring subtle environmental issues. She spoke of feeling "suffocated" by a hot shower if she used a perfumed soap, of frantically trying to buy the "magic, right crackers" to end her relentless nausea and vomiting, of trying to "power eat" during her better moments to make up for lost meals. Her nose was so sensitive she could smell the cardboard boxes when she opened the kitchen cupboards at home.

Dagmar was visited several times by the hospital psychiatrist, who investigated her commitment to her pregnancy. Each time he said, "Well, she says she wants the baby . . . but I wonder what else is going on at home."

In trying to pinpoint factors contributing to the waxing and waning course of her morning sickness in the hospital, Dagmar commented that every time she looked better, her doctor or nurse expected her to run laps around the floor. She found herself losing ground when she did laps just before her wing of the hospital received meal trays, or when the housekeepers' dirty water buckets came too close.

One weekend a part-time nurse told Dagmar to empty her own emesis (vomit) basin after measuring and recording the contents on the "I/O" (intake/output) sheet. Shortly thereafter, Dagmar overheard a conversation between this older nurse and a student nurse. "I just hate emptying emesis basins," the older nurse said. "It always makes me sick and I start to gag. I make them do it. After all, they have to do it at home. They should be used to it by now!"

According to this nurse, the patient was also to measure her urine, recording that amount as well. Dagmar found the smell of her concentrated urine obnoxious. But she did not have the courage or stamina to tell the nurse that these tasks bordered on torture.

During one admission, Dagmar had a double room and a roommate with the same problem. The other woman told Dagmar she had decided to terminate the pregnancy, a much-wanted one, because her two-year-old daughter was being passed from relative to relative with the various hospitalizations. Finding reliable and safe child care was becoming a major problem. The roommate's job also did not offer sick time benefits, and she was losing a substantial amount of money because she couldn't work. When one of the roommate's coworkers came to visit, she said cutbacks at the office were coming. Not knowing when she was going to get better, Dagmar's roommate felt she had no choice but to end the pregnancy.

With adequate hydration and hyperalimentation Dagmar eventually recovered some of her lost strength. As her hydration improved, she found herself having French toast, root beer, and layer cake every morning for breakfast, despite her interest in good nutrition. This new breakfast combination proved mysteriously successful. Once she'd achieved the goal of eating and not vomiting for three days, the feeding line was removed from her neck and she was discharged. After her discharge, we spoke occasionally on the phone; not until month 8 did she feel well. At that point she started to work ceaselessly trying to make up for the months of no productivity. Her second daughter was born two weeks after her due date. Dagmar's comment: "Does it look like this is an unwanted baby?"

Ellenmarie

An efficient, precise librarian at a major university, Ellenmarie spent the majority of both of her pregnancies in the hospital. Starting off at 5 feet, 3 inches and 112 pounds, she lost 15 or 20 pounds in her first pregnancy. She regained the lost weight ten months after the pregnancy was over.

Getting pregnant again was not in Ellenmarie's immediate plan, since she felt she had not recovered from her first "motherhood" ordeal. However, Ellenmarie discovered her unplanned second pregnancy one day while she was changing her daughter's diaper: she became instantly ill. By the following week, she was unable to function in her job, noting that the smell of musty books and manuscripts "made me continually nauseous and if I wasn't gagging then I'd be vomiting."

Hospitalized on a high-risk pregnancy unit, she made little

improvement, except that "the moldy smell was gone." Her nurses, nutritionist, and doctors all tried to feed her without success, and she finally refused to hear about or talk about food, since the mere mention of it was unsettling. She noted that certain sights added to her queasiness, like the busy necktie her doctor wore. Noises became more acute than usual.

When she finally began to eat, she learned self-hypnosis to "try to keep the food down." She noted that "the minute my baby was delivered, I could eat!" She asked for and received two roast beef dinners, which she ate. "I told them one was for my husband, but I just knew I was going to be able to chow it right down—and I did!"

Fabianna

Dubbed "Mrs. Lemonade and potato chips" by her father, Fabianna was hospitalized on four separate occasions and spent a total of thirty days in the hospital. During the fourth stay, of nineteen days, her diet consisted mainly of lemonade frappes and potato chips, both of which were roundly criticized by her family. Up to this time, Fabianna said, her coworkers had thought she was just "putting it on" when she complained of nausea and vomiting. Her weight had dropped twenty pounds in twelve weeks and she was no longer able to function at home or in her office.

During one hospital admission her doctor, an avid sailor, saw an ad in a boating magazine about antiseasickness wristbands. He gave Fabianna the clipping, saying it was worth a gamble. She ordered a set and had them delivered at once. A bead on the band was supposed to exert pressure on a nerve which, according to the brochure, was connected to the vomiting center in the brain. The speculation was that the pressure controlled the urge to vomit.

In two days Fabianna felt better than she had in weeks. She said she felt foolish wearing the scratchy yellow bands on her wrists, but for whatever reason, she made progress. After maintaining stability for two days, she was ready for discharge.

Meanwhile, her mother was busy cleaning the young couple's apartment. When she entered the spotless rooms and smelled the cleaning agents, Fabianna immediately felt nauseated again. She opened a window and stuck her head out for fresh air. She asked her husband to remove all the pails and bottles of cleaning materials immediately. She told me, "I know my mother didn't understand—she was only trying to help—but the smells were really getting to me. I knew if I started vomiting I'd be right back in that hospital."

Fabianna's relatives bet the baby would be a girl with lots of hair. According to an old wives' tale, the hair of the unborn fetus aggravates the mother's gastrointestinal tract and causes vomiting. Fabianna's husband's family had heard that morning sickness was the result of the "double estrogen theory"—the notion that a baby girl's own estrogen is what makes the mother sick.

During her months of waiting, Fabianna was able to return to work part-time. She said she had to open the bus windows in the dead of winter to get gulps of fresh air. Once an older man tried to close the window and she said simply, "I have really bad morning sickness and I'm trying not to get sick." He apologized and moved his seat. She also found that when she rode on the bus, she had to look straight ahead, as sitting sideways made her instantly queasy. Once on the subway, she felt that too many people were jammed in and "robbed me of my air." She leaped out at the next stop, seconds before vomiting into a trash can, while peeling off her jacket and scarf, perspiring despite the cold.

Finally the time came when Fabianna and her husband become proud parents—of a baby boy. Fabianna, who admits that she wondered many times while she was vomiting and retching with morning sickness, "Why did I ever want to be pregnant?" now says, "My baby is so wonderful, cheerful, happy . . . I guess the end had to turn out good because the beginning and the middle were just so horrible." To this day, the reason for the success of the lemonade frappes and potato chips remains a mystery.

Gracie

Tall, attractive, athletic, and professionally accomplished describe Gracie. When she was admitted for care in the early weeks of her first pregnancy, she reported comments others had made to her. She was a research (not in prenatal nutrition) nutritionist, and most of her friends, nonpregnant colleagues, and family wondered why she couldn't take care of herself well enough to avoid hospitalization. She quickly read up on morning sickness, but found very little information that discussed what to do if soda crackers failed.

Once Gracie had been hospitalized, we explored the role of various smells in her state of well-being. Gracie thought of certain odors at home that sent her over the edge. The smell of cooking pasta, she could say with certainty, was a problem. The solution was for her husband to cook the pasta at his mother's house and bring it home to heat in a microwave.

Another problem was the family dog, who suddenly smelled more "doggy" to Gracie. The friendly sixty-pound Collie would follow Gracie to the bathroom, often keeping her company during a bout of vomiting. To Gracie's husband the dog smelled no different now than ever before, and he was upset that the immediate solution meant Gracie and the dog couldn't be in the same room.

Five feet, 8 inches tall, Gracie started her pregnancy at about 115 pounds and hit a low of 98 pounds when she was hospitalized, for a loss of 17 pounds. Because she ran a slight fever for three days after her admission, Gracie's doctors sent her for an endoscopy to rule out an ulcer and also sent her for an ultrasound scan of her gallbladder, which showed "sludge." "Sludge" in the gallbladder is a common finding in pregnancy, and is a concentrated form of bile, especially when nausea and vomiting are present because of being somewhat dehydrated.

The endoscopy required that a small tube be inserted down Gracie's throat, which was anesthesized with a xylocaine spray. Through the tube, the radiologist could view the interior of Gracie's stomach, which was normal. As Gracie feared, she gagged through a good part of the examination. Luckily her nausea did not escalate into vomiting.

Hospitalized for about a week and then home for another three and a half weeks, Gracie returned to work part-time. She would drive into the city after rush hour to minimize the likelihood of getting behind a garbage truck or bus. She avoided bumpy roads and sudden stops. When her husband drove, Gracie was told to remind him that bumps and jolts might be trigger factors and to drive carefully.

She brought lunch to work: marshmallow Rice Krispies squares, baked potatoes, and vanilla yogurt. This was a far cry from her former choices of whole-wheat pita, skim milk, and vegetarian salad with chick-peas.

During the pregnancy, Gracie kept a diary of events and noted comments made by well-meaning friends and relatives while she was sick. Two of the most irritating comments were "Just use positive thinking, it'll go away" and "Oh, you *have* to eat something." A friend took Gracie's husband aside and offered this advice: "You just have to be ruthless and make her eat!" Gracie reflected, "When you're nauseous half the time and vomiting the other half, the last thing you care to read about is the basic food groups and how eating a few crackers will fix you right up!"

After twenty-three weeks, Gracie started to feel normal again and began to gain weight. At forty weeks her weight was up to 130 pounds, for a gain of 32 pounds from her lowest weight. Despite more speculations that the baby had to be a girl because she was so sick, Gracie delivered via cesarean section an 8-pound, 4-ounce baby boy.

Hazel

Tall and stately at 5 feet, 5 inches tall and 115 pounds, this native of Trinidad experienced nausea and vomiting with all three of her pregnancies. In the late 1970s, when she was pregnant for the first time, she suffered from morning sickness for the first four months. During the midwinter months her weight dipped to 100 pounds. She experienced a first-trimester intolerance of milk products. A more difficult situation to manage was her excess saliva and constant desire to spit. Her first daughter was born full-term, at five pounds, eight ounces.

Two years later, Hazel was pregnant again. From day one, it was a battle to control the nausea and vomiting. Smells, perfumes, and cooking oils were all triggers. Starving all day long, she often had enough appetite and desire to eat by the late afternoon if her mother cooked favorite Trinidadian dishes of salted fish with boiled potatoes or salty pig-tail soup.

Milk, one of her favorite foods, was out of the question. At one point she vomited blood and was hospitalized for dehydration for a week. She luckily was put in a private room. Her weight dropped 25 pounds, from 115 to 90, during the worst of the crisis. This pregnancy ended with delivery at seven months. Weighing three pounds, eight ounces, Hazel's second daughter spent one month in the hospital's neonatal intensive care unit and was discharged without problems.

Eight years later, the third pregnancy was punctuated by what Hazel described as "the worst case!" Her prepregnancy weight was 119 pounds and dipped 10 pounds during the worst phase. Smells again were a problem. One successful remedy she discovered was Enos, an antacid from "the Islands" that she bought in her ethnic fruit store. After the morning ritual of Enos, she could keep down some soy milk, hot or cold. Boiling it, she could take it to work with her in a Thermos. Another meal would be a soft scrambled egg, made with soy milk, packed and eaten at work with a salty sausage.

Hazel always drove her own car, saying that bus drivers would bristle if she wanted to get off at an unscheduled stop. Again, at home, whether for lunch or dinner, she was able to eat if her mother cooked. A frequent meal was highly salted fish, sautéed tomatoes with onions and green bananas, with a potato or a yam as a side dish. Another usual meal was the pig-tail soup, highly salted, green, and somewhat lumpy; ingredients included split peas, chopped potatoes, and carrots.

For some unexplained reason, Hazel could cook for her household but was unable to eat. Eating at someone else's home, however, was remarkably successful as long as the menu offered varieties of curried meat (beef, chicken, and goat), salty chicken-foot soup, tripe soup, or "pilah." Pilah was described as a mixture of pigeon peas, rice, and beef or chicken. Hazel's secret seasonings included soy sauce, garlic powder, garlic salt, hot pepper, and chili. Hazel's mother included all the same spices, but added ginger and a bay leaf.

Although Hazel had read that rosemary tea was supposed to settle the stomach, it didn't work for her. Her beverage of choice was ice-cold grapefruit juice or sorrel tea. She brewed dried sorrel leaves, steeping them for twenty-four hours after sugar and clove had been added. Consumed hot or cold, sorrel tea worked.

Another successful and favorite island beverage was "Marby," made from the bark of a tree boiled with aniseed. After it was brewed, sugar and angostura bitters were added. As it aged, it became stronger, so water was periodically added to the storage container in the refrigerator.

Hazel's third and final pregnancy again concluded at seven months. Her weight, however, recovered from the low of 109 pounds to 139 pounds at delivery. Her 5-pound, 12-ounce son was hospitalized for two days of observation and then went home with his mother.

Iona

A happily married woman with three children, stunning Iona looked as if nothing ever went awry in her life. But she'd been sick with her first pregnancy. She thought it couldn't happen again with her second, but it did. It was during her third pregnancy that she reported many of the details of her capricious morning sickness.

One of the first things she noted was a constant weird taste in her mouth, and she became very concerned about the freshness of her breath. Like all the other women, she found the breath of other people difficult to endure. She noted that oddly, she felt more at ease if her stomach seemed empty rather than full. However, she did eat and gain the appropriate thirty pounds during her pregnancy.

In contrast to her two previous pregnancies, this time she wanted food after she vomited. She loved the theory of "Radar Nose" and found that the slightest scent could set off queasiness. Her description was perfect: she felt like a volcano ready to fire up and out. This time around, she found that Di-Gel antacid tablets worked best for her heartburn. Her tactile senses were escalated as well. Pressure on her navel created nausea, but she found a solution. She made a small pad of gauze and put it over her navel with surgical tape.

After eating, Iona found that lying on her right side propped up by two pillows was helpful. The nausea and vomiting lasted her whole pregnancy, except for a short respite in the second trimester. At that time, she craved strong, spicy foods. Tacos, nachos, dips, chips, BBQ ribs, onion rings, and stuffed clams were items her husband, Mark, learned to procure "yesterday." Iona also gravitated to cinnamon, ginger, almond, nutmeg, and fennel seeds as stomach settlers. She ate popcorn and bacon, lettuce, and tomato sandwiches for a while, but once they lost their effect, they were off the menu for the duration.

The only two foods that Iona could always tolerate, through all three pregnancies, were cold lobster salad and shrimp salad smothered in lemon juice. Beef and pork were definitely out.

She also noted that fatigue and extremes of temperature set her off. She always got sick whenever she began to shiver or sweat. Because her rest was disturbed often, she had trouble with migraine headaches.

A brief trial of vitamin B6 proved futile. She switched brands of prenatal vitamins, as they seemed only to make the nausea worse. She took her folate tablets and Ferrous Sequels with orange juice, which surprisingly did not cause any discomfort. Iona said she developed "iatrogenic constipation" because there were too many people in her household for too few bathrooms; she endured a failed attempt with FiberCon, which only caused bloating.

Iona felt dizzy much of the time, and her doctor commented frequently that her blood pressure was low. Though she felt "green" up to month 9, it all ended with the birth of her third child, a healthy girl.

All of these women suffered from severe morning sickness, but many aspects of their experience are echoed in the stories of women whose morning sickness is milder or confined to the first trimester. Perhaps some of their techniques will work for you.

CHAPTER 14

Thoughts from the
Other Side

At a time when the whole world should look bright and rosy, couples who are attempting to cope with the problems of nausea and vomiting during pregnancy find few resources available to them. This chapter is included almost as a postscript to the preceding chapter. It contains the comments of husbands and partners of women whom I've interviewed and should provide some insight into the issues and problems they encountered as they waited to become fathers.

David

"Does lightning ever strike twice in the same spot?" David asked. Having endured morning sickness with his wife's first pregnancy, he thought it couldn't happen again. Among the issues he tried to deal with was a continuing feeling of helplessness. He often wondered what he would do if, while on his evening job as a hotel manager, he received an emergency call from his wife, Laura. During her bouts of severe vomiting, Laura was unable to look after their two-year-old son, Leif. Laura would put him into his crib to keep him safe and call David, begging him to come home to help her get Leif ready for bed because she was unable to manage by herself.

David found concentrating at work difficult because he knew things were probably in shambles at home. Three times during the second pregnancy Laura was hospitalized, leaving Leif with David's parents. "After this pregnancy is over, that's it!" David announced. Both of them agreed that the difficulties involved were just overwhelming, and they decided on permanent birth control.

Michael

Like David, Michael was a second-time father. With the first pregnancy, he'd been surprised to find that morning sickness lasted as long as it did, since all the books about pregnancy Rita had bought said it should be over after the first trimester. His private concern about his wife's health and the baby mounted with every passing day of her nausea. When the nausea finally ended after five months, Michael felt as if a lifetime had passed.

With the second pregnancy, he expected morning sickness. His main concern every day was getting their three-year-old, Mandi, dressed and to the caretaker of the day. When Michael and Mandi visited Rita in the hospital, where she was receiving intravenous fluids, Mandi clung to her father's pant leg, afraid of "those tubes." She preferred to see "the babies" at the other end of the ward. Michael said visiting and spending time with his wife was impossible because he was always running after Mandi. He admits that when his wife came home, the most difficult task he faced was emptying her emesis basin.

Tom

Another man whose wife endured morning sickness during two pregnancies, Tom found the comments by his relatives the most difficult part of the experience to handle. His mother, a very traditional woman, was horrified that her daughter-in-law, Mimi, was not cooking dinners for her son. The family gossiped, whispering, "Oh, she can't be *that* sick!" The couple's first child, Scotty, was often cared for by Mimi's mother. Only when Mimi ended up in the hospital with major complications of gallbladder disease in pregnancy, on top of severe morning sickness, was the seriousness of her ordeal recognized by other family members.

Their second baby, Andrew, weighed in at 7 pounds, 3 ounces.

But Mimi's predelivery weight was 40 pounds less than her pre-pregnancy weight of 165 pounds. The stress and strain of the nine-month struggle were evident to everyone who knew Mimi as a fun-loving, high-energy woman. Eight weeks later, Mimi entered the hospital for a two-day stay to have her gallbladder removed. Tom said it seemed a lot easier for the relatives to understand a gallbladder problem than morning sickness.

William

Excited about his wife's first pregnancy, William never expected morning sickness. He was surprised when, early in the pregnancy, he had to drive his wife, Maryann, to the emergency room of the nearby hospital for intravenous hydration. This worked for one day. The second visit was an overnighter on the high-risk obstetrical unit. Here William learned that the morning sickness might be short-lived or might last through the entire pregnancy.

A two-income couple, they'd had their lives planned up until the birth of the baby. With the potential problem of one lost income, they needed to examine their financial situation. William found the anxiety of "not knowing how it will all go" incompatible with his expectations. They cut back on weekly expenses, such as a health-club membership, and bought a less expensive second car. Morning sickness did not fit into William's "life plan," and he found this very stressful. To reduce numerous trips to the grocery store after he got home from work, William invested in a cellular phone and called home once on the road home.

Alan

When Alan and Claire received the "official" news that she was pregnant, they had already endured a week of sporadic nausea and vomiting. Soon after, Claire spent a weekend in the hospital. Alan's method of coping was to begin smoking again, after a hiatus of six years. He found talking to people unhelpful and believed that very few understood what he was experiencing—almost everyone seemed to think "it was *just* morning sickness." He spent all his free time visiting Claire in the hospital. Too worried to relax, he avoided direct questions from family and friends and would often change the subject.

After this experience, Alan had some advice for other men: "Talk to your wife about your feelings, about the baby, and about the pregnancy. There will be time in the future for happiness and fun, but do not expect anything for a while until your wife is feeling better."

C H A P T E R 15

Recipes and Menus

What you eat can make the difference between feeling miserable and feeling stable or at least "less worse," as many women say. Women with morning sickness I've treated have found that the recipes given here worked for them. You may want to reread Chapter 5, "Managing Morning Sickness with Food," before you decide which recipes to try.

In gathering these recipes, I used the foods characteristics approach discussed in Chapter 5. If you don't know what particular food you want, these prompts are often helpful:

salty	spicy
crunchy	liquid
fruity	hot
sour	tart
smooth	solid
bland	cold
bitter	tangy
wet	lumpy
earthy	temperate
sweet	fizzy
dry	or whatever

Food descriptors are very subjective; you may decide to reclassify these recipes under different headings.

In the matter of taste, certain areas of the tongue have been identified as sending certain messages. Refer to the chart on page 181 and see whether this "road map" holds true for you. Note the two areas labeled "vagus nerve." Touching this area often elicits a gag reflex.

Hospital (or clinical) registered dietitians often supplement regular food, trying to boost calories or the nutritional profile. To boost protein intake, a product called "ProMod" is available from Ross Laboratories (Columbus, OH 43216). Although it adds 5 grams of protein per 5-gram scoop, it is not a balanced diet. It can be added to mashed potatoes and other soft, bland foods. Polycose (glucose polymers, also from Ross Laboratories) is a clear liquid which adds carbohydrate calories. Each tablespoon, or 15 cc, of Polycose can add 30 tasteless calories to tea or juice. To change the texture of foods, ThickenUp can be added. A thin juice can be changed to the consistency of nectar or pudding, which may be better tolerated. This product is fortified with eighteen essential vitamins and minerals and slightly changes the taste of certain foods. (ThickenUp is made by Sandoz Nutrition, 5320 West Twenty-third Street, P.O. Box 370, Minneapolis, NM 55440.) Please note that several products are available which do essentially the same thing as the above. Consult a registered dietitian for the best way to use them.)

When I feed a woman with morning sickness, I ask two main questions about whether a food or beverage is successful in ending a crisis: is it (1) driving a thirst or (2) settling a queasy stomach? It's not surprising to find a woman going back and forth with choices.

Orange Fruit Pudding
(TART)

MAKES 4 SERVINGS

2 cups fresh orange juice (or 2 cups grapefruit juice)
2 sweet oranges, peeled and sectioned (or 2 large grapefruits)
2 tbsp cornstarch

Put cornstarch in saucepan and add small amount of juice, stirring until all blended. Heat and stir in rest of juice. Cook until thickened. Cool slightly. Stir in orange or grapefruit sections. Chill in individual dessert cups or in a large bowl.

Per serving: calories, 98; cholesterol (CHO), 23 g; protein (PRO), 1 g; fat, 0 g; water, 86%

Characteristics: high vitamin C tartness, which can be adjusted, high amount of built-in fluid, fiber source, good source of potassium

Charger

(BITTER)

Add 2 dashes Angostura bitters and lime wedge to a tall glass. Add sparkling water and ice.

Characteristics: tanginess can be adjusted, fizzy and cold

Pumpkin-Cheese Pie

(SMOOTH/BLAND)

MAKES 8 SERVINGS

8-inch ready to fill graham cracker pie shell, or used gingerbread crackers
1 cup cooked or canned plain pumpkin
3 eggs or the equivalent in egg substitute
1 tbsp rum flavoring or vanilla extract
pinch of salt
¼ cup brown sugar
1½ cups low-fat creamed cottage cheese
1½ t pumpkin pie spices, or your preference of nutmeg, cinnamon and allspice

Preheat oven to 275 degrees before beginning preparation. Combine all ingredients, except pie shell, in a blender and blend on high speed until very smooth. Pour into pie shell and bake for 1 hour or more, until filling is set. Chill before serving.

Per serving: calories, 310; CHO, 36 g; PRO, 9 g; fat, 14 g

Characteristics: high protein, can eat hot or cold, can adjust spiciness, high calcium item, good source of vitamin A

Flan

(BLAND/SMOOTH)

MAKES 6 SERVINGS

1¾ **cups sugar**
6 **eggs or equivalent in egg substitutes or half and half**
2 **cups milk**
1 **t vanilla**
¼ **t cinnamon**

Place 1 cup sugar in the bottom of a glass pie plate and place in preheated 350 degree oven for about 20 minutes, or until sugar is caramelized. Remove from oven and cool to room temperature.

Beat eggs with remaining sugar and gradually beat in milk. Add vanilla and cinnamon. Stir well.

Put pie plate with the caramelized sugar in a large pan, filled with ½" warm water. Pour the egg-milk mixture over caramelized sugar. Bake in preheated oven at 350 degrees for about ½ hour. Cool to room temperature. Invert onto shallow dish.

Variations:

1) Add grated peel of 1 orange to milk mixture
2) Add ¼ cup shredded coconut to milk mixture
3) Substitute almond extract for vanilla
4) Add 2 tbsps cocoa to milk mixture

Per serving: calories, 340; CHO, 62 g; PRO, 9 g; fat, 7 g; water, 60%

Characteristics: can vary taste, smooth, bland, high calorie, high protein, can eat hot or cold, good source of calcium, phosphorus

Carrot Raisin Salad
(CRUNCHY)

MAKES 4 SERVINGS.

1 cup grated carrots
1½ tbsp raisins
1 tbsp lemon juice
1 tbsp mayonnaise

Mix all ingredients together and chill.

Per serving; calories, 48; CHO, 6 g; PRO, 0 g; fat, 3 g

Characteristics: high iron, high fiber, high built-in water content, can add nuts, crushed pineapple, etc.

Rice-Carrot Casserole
(BLAND)

MAKES 8 SERVINGS

2 cups partially cooked white or brown rice (start with 1 cup raw)
2–3 raw carrots
1 large onion chopped
1 clove garlic, minced
2 eggs beaten, or equivalent in egg substitute
2–3 tbsp safflower oil
2 t salt
¼ cup dry skim milk powder

Preheat oven. Stir all ingredients together and pour into an oiled 7" x 7" pan and bake for 45 minutes to one hour. If desired, add 1 cup of grated cheese to hot topping if desired.

Per serving: calories, 140; CHO, 19 g; PRO, 4 g; fat, 5 g; water, 76%

Characteristics: high fiber, vegetarian, high vitamin A

Cranberry Salad

(CRUNCHY/TART)

MAKES 8 SERVINGS

1 cup chopped cranberries
¾ cup sugar
1 pkg. lemon Jell-O
1 cup hot water
1 cup crushed pineapple
1 cup pineapple juice (drained from the above)
1 cup chopped celery

Combine cranberries and sugar. Dissolve Jell-O in hot water, add pineapple juice. Chill until partially set. Add cranberry mixture, pineapple, walnuts and chopped celery. Spoon into Jell-O mold. Chill until firm.

Per serving: calories, 120; CHO, 30 g; PRO, 1 g; fat, 0 g; fiber, 1.3 g; water, 75%

Characteristics: high fiber, high water content

Noodle Kugel

(BLAND/CRUNCHY)

MAKES **8** SERVINGS

1 lb of cooked noodles
16 oz of low-fat cottage cheese
4 eggs, or equivalent egg substitute
1 cup low-fat plain yogurt
1 cup golden raisins
½ cup brown sugar
4 tbsp melted margarine
1½ t vanilla extract
½ t cinnamon

Combine all ingredients in a pre-greased ovenproof dish.
Refrigerate overnight.

Top with 1 tablespoon margarine and sprinkle with
cinnamon.

Bake in preheated 350 degree oven for 1½ hours, or until
golden brown on top.

Per serving: calories, 335; CHO, 48 g; PRO, 15 g; fat, 10 g; water, 63%

Characteristics: bland, variable add-ins, high protein, high calcium, can eat
hot or cold, good source of vitamin B12

Rice Water

(BLAND/COLD)

MAKES 2–3 SERVINGS

1 tbsp rice
2 cups cold water or milk
1 teaspoon sugar
cinnamon, nutmeg, orange and lemon peel for flavoring

Put rice into a pan with water or milk and cook over moderate heat. Bring to boil and then simmer for 30 minutes. Strain, and add sugar, spice or peel as you want. (Or can cool and blend rice and liquid in blender for added calories and thickness.) Chill and serve.

Per serving (calculations based on half milk, half water): calories, 53; CHO, 8 g; PRO, 3 g; fat, 1 g

Characteristics: make with water if milk gives you gastrointestinal problems, variable flavorings, can make ahead, high energy bland drink

Prune Whip
(BLAND/SMOOTH)
MAKES 6 SERVINGS

16 pitted prunes
3 small pieces of lemon rind
1½ cups water
2 egg whites, beaten stiff
1 t lemon juice

Soak prunes and lemon rind in water for 1 hour. Simmer for 20–30 minutes, until fruit is soft. If necessary, add more water. Let cool. Puree in blender. Fold in beaten eggs whites into prune puree and add lemon juice. Chill for at least an hour.

Per serving: calories, 35; CHO, 8 g; PRO, 1 g; fat, 0 g

Characteristics: high iron, built-in water content

Waldorf Salad
(CRUNCHY/TART)
MAKES 4 SERVINGS

4 medium sized tart red apples with peels, cored and diced
¾ cup finely chopped celery
½ cup coarsely chopped walnuts
⅔ cup calorie reduced mayonnaise or plain yogurt
add sprinkle of cinnamon, nutmeg if desired

Stir all ingredients together. To hold mixture together, add more yogurt as needed. Cover and chill for at least 2–3 hours. Serve on lettuce leaves.

Per serving: calories, 245; CHO, 37 g; PRO, 6 g; fat, 10 g; water, 80%

Characteristics: high fiber, tart, can vary taste and contents by adding chopped dates, red or green grapes, substitute fresh pears for apples

Honeydew Soup
(TANGY)

MAKES 4 (¾-CUP) SERVINGS

1 large honeydew melon
1 tbsp corn-oil margarine
3 tbsp minced onion
salt and pepper to taste
2 tbsp chopped mixture of chervil, chives, and parsley

1. Seed melon and cut into large chunks.
2. In medium saucepan, heat margarine and sauté onion until soft. Remove from heat and stir in melon cubes.
3. Add salt and pepper if desired.
4. Puree mixture in blender or food processor and refrigerate several hours or overnight before serving.
5. Garnish with herb mixture.

Per serving: calories, 140; CHO, 30 g; PRO, 2 g; fat, 3 g; water, 89%

Characteristics: tangy, high water content, high potassium

A note about "lemon therapy": I have found in my practice that lemons are soothing and reduce nausea for all sorts of patients who suffer from nausea, obstetrical as well as chemotherapy. I suggest they do with the lemons whatever they like—scratching the skin and just smelling them; cutting them in half and licking the surface; eating them like oranges, with or without salt; or tying them inside a scarf for a fragrance necklace.

The literature cautions against eating lemons for fear of ruining dental enamel. I've found that lemons can help break a cycle of nausea and vomiting and vomiting is no less damaging to dental enamel. For most women, once the crisis is over, other foods begin to appeal again.

If you like lemon you'll probably love my world-famous lemon mousse. I refer to the texture of this mousse as a "solid liquid." It's a favorite among my patients.

Lemon Mousse
(SMOOTH/TANGY)

MAKES 2 SERVINGS

Make a small package of lemon gelatin according to directions. Let it set up in refrigerator. Put 1 cup of the gelatin into blender, followed by ½ cup hard vanilla ice cream. Whirl for about 10 seconds, or until color blended.

Per serving: calories, 180; CHO, 30 g; PRO, 4 g; fat, 6 g; water, 76%

Characteristics: a "solid liquid"

Indian Rice Porridge
(BLAND)

MAKES 6 (½-CUP) SERVINGS

3 cups low-fat milk
1 cup Basmati rice
1 medium egg
⅓ cup sugar (or less)
¼ t salt
¼ t almond extract

1. Put 2 cups of milk into medium saucepan and add rice.
2. Cook slowly until liquid is almost absorbed.
3. Beat egg into the remaining 1 cup of milk and add sugar.
4. Add egg mixture slowly to mixture in saucepan, stirring constantly.
5. Add extract.
6. Serve hot or cold.

Per serving: calories, 228; CHO, 42 g; PRO, 7 g; fat, 4 g; water, 70%

Characteristics: reheats well in microwave, high-calcium, high-protein, pleasant essence

Grated Finnish Vegetable Salad
(BITTER)
MAKES 8 SERVINGS (1/2-CUP)

VEGETABLES:

1 cup grated carrots
1 cup grated rutabaga or white turnips
1 cup grated raw beets
1 cup grated apples
1 cup grated red or green cabbage

Mix ingredients together and arrange on a large plate.

DRESSING:

¼ cup freshly squeezed lemon juice
½ cup orange juice
1 t oil
¼ cup chopped parsley

Mix together and pour over vegetables.

Mix together and serve separately ¼ cup grated horseradish and ½ cup sour cream (try the new light variety).

Per serving: calories, 77; CHO, 13 g; PRO, 2 g; fat, 3 g; water, 87%

Characteristics: unusual taste, high fiber content, high potassium and vitamin C content

Easy Cheesy Noodles
(BLAND)

MAKES **4** SERVINGS

This recipe is used with permission of Nancy Clark, R.D., MS, from her book, *Nancy Clark's Sports Nutrition Cookbook* (Champaign, Illinois: Leisure Press, 1990).

I like this recipe for its versatility. The nutrient profile is based on adding ½ cup diced tomato, ½ cup freshly chopped and cooked broccoli, and ½ cup al dente julienne carrots, which makes a very colorful dish.

8 oz dry egg noodles
1 tbsp olive oil
6 oz low-fat cheese (munster for a blander meal, blue cheese or sharp cheese for tangy taste)
Optional: salt, pepper, dried mustard, parsley, garlic powder, Italian seasonsing, diced tomatoes, steamed broccoli, peas, julienne carrots

1. Cook noodles according to package directions and drain.
2. Add oil, cheese, and other ingredients of your choice.

Per serving: calories, 365; CHO, 32 g; PRO, 17 g; fat, 19 g; water, 66%

Characteristics: quick to fix, high fiber, high potassium and calcium content, good source of vitamin A, very flexible recipe

Fruit and Vegetable Salad

(COLD)

MAKES 4 (½-CUP) SERVINGS

1. Grate 2 carrots (1 cup) and 1 apple (1 cup) together.
2. Add ½ cup chopped parsley.
3. Combine 3 tbsp lemon juice, 1 tbsp oil (optional), and 1 t sugar (if desired) and pour over mixture. Toss and served chilled.

Per serving: calories, 80; CHO, 13 g; PRO, 1 g; fat, 3 g; water, 82%

Characteristics: high fiber content, high folic acid and potassium, refreshing taste and texture

Potato Crunchies

(CRUNCHY)

MAKES 2 (½-CUP) SERVINGS

1. Peel a large potato and shred in food processor. Put into a strainer and rinse with cold water. Pat dry with paper towels.
2. Heat nonstick frying pan coated with small amount of fresh oil or cooking spray. Add potato shreds and sauté until brown and crispy.
3. Season as you choose with salt, pepper, parmesan cheese, or vinegar.

Per serving: calories, 72 g; CHO, 17 g; PRO, 2 g; fat, 1 g; water, 75%

Characteristics: high potassium, interesting taste and texture, can be made spicier or saltier

Blueberry Soup
(FRUITY)

MAKES 6 (⅔-CUP) SERVINGS

2 pints washed blueberries
3 cups water
¼ cup sugar (or to taste)
1½ tbsp potato starch
¼ cup cold water

1. Put blueberries and 3 cups water into medium saucepan, bring to a boil, reduce heat and simmer for 10 minutes. Do not boil. Season with sugar and remove from heat.
2. Mix potato starch with water, making smooth paste. Slowly pour into mixture, stirring constantly with whisk. Bring to a quick boil and remove from heat.
3. Serve warm or cold, with or without sugar sprinkled on top.

Per serving: calories, 70 g; CHO, 17 g; PRO, 1 g; fat, 1 g; water, 90%

Characteristics: thick liquid, easily digestible carboydrates

Cauliflower Walnut Casserole

(EARTHY)

MAKES 4 LARGE SERVINGS

This is one of my favorite recipes and is used with the
permission of two creative women, Linda Hackfeld, R.D.,
M.P.H., and Betsy Eykyn, M.S. who wrote *Cooking a la Heart*.
This book is a must-have, with piles of interesting, different,
easy-to-make recipes. $20 postpaid from Appletree Press, Inc.,
Good Council Drive, Suite 125, Mankato, MN 56001.

Some women have reported that a plate with a lot of colors
can increase their nausea—they prefer light/white/tan foods
during this time. Have someone make this dish for you because
preparation time is slightly extended. When you reheat, use low
heat.

1 medium head cauliflower, broken into florets
1 cup low-fat plain yogurt
1 cup shredded cheddar cheese
1 tbsp flour
2 t low-sodium chicken-flavored bouillon granules
1 t dry mustard
⅓ cup chopped walnuts
⅓ cup dry bread crumbs
1 tbsp margarine
1 t dried crushed marjoram

1. In medium saucepan, cook cauliflower in water, drain, and
   put into 10-by-6-inch baking dish.
2. Mix yogurt, cheese, flour, bouillon granules, and mustard
   and pour over cauliflower.
3. Mix walnuts, bread crumbs, margarine, and marjoram
   together and sprinkle on top. Bake for about 20 minutes
   in a preheated 400°F oven.

Per serving: calories, 330; CHO, 25 g; PRO, 17 g; fat, 20 g; water, 80%

Characteristics: lightly colored but tasty and nutritious, high fiber and
potassium content, good amount of calcium, folic acid, vitamin C, niacin

Wild-Rice Pilaf

(EARTHY)

MAKES 6 (½-CUP) SERVINGS

2 cups strong chicken broth (preferably homemade)
1 small finely chopped onion
1 clove of garlic, chopped or crushed in garlic press
1 t finely minced fresh lemon rind
1 cup wild rice
½ cup brown rice
2 tbsp toasted sesame seeds

1. Heat ½ cup broth in large saucepan. When it boils, add onion and garlic, cooking until soft.
2. Add lemon rind and both rices, along with the rest of the broth. Reduce heat and simmer for 1 to 1¼ hours or until rice is just tender. (You can also put the mixture in an ovenproof covered dish and bake for 1 hour.)
3. Just before serving, stir in sesame seeds.

Per serving: calories, 150; CHO, 26 g; PRO, 6 g; fat, 3 g; water, 78%

Characteristics: reheats well, high fiber, crunchy texture

Peanut Butter Pudding

(EARTHY)

MAKES 4 (3-OZ) SERVINGS

1½ tbsp chunky peanut butter
8 oz evaporated skim milk
1 egg plus 1 egg white
¼ t vanilla

1. Blend all ingredients together until smooth.
2. Place 4 small ramekins in a large baking dish which has been filled with 1 inch of hot water.
3. Pour mixture evenly into ramekins and bake at 350°F for about 45 minutes.

Per serving: calories, 105; CHO, 8 g; PRO, 8 g; fat, 4 g; water, 73%

Characteristics: smooth, high nutritional value, high calcium, high potassium

Different Shake

(EARTHY)

MAKES 1 (8-OZ) SERVING OR 3 (2½-OZ) POPSICLES

1 medium peach, or 2 canned peach halves
2 oz soft tofu
6 small ice cubes, or 4 large ones
¼ cup lemonade
⅛ t lemon extract
1 tbsp wheat germ
½ t ground cinnamon

Put all ingredients in blender. Blend until smooth. Serve at once or pour mixture into popsicle molds and freeze.

Per serving: calories, 135; CHO, 22 g; PRO, 7 g; fat, 4 g; water, 84%

Characteristics: quick to fix, high fiber, high protein and calories

Banana-Peanut Power Shake
(EARTHY)

MAKES 1 (8-OZ) SERVING

I know that most blender manufacturers say never put ice in a blender, but I've been abusing my blender for years and it's still whirring away.

4 oz honey vanilla yogurt
2 tbsp peanut butter
1 ripe banana
3 tbsp nonfat dry milk
6 small ice cubes, or 4 large ones

Place ingredients in blender in order listed. Blend until all ice is crushed. Serve immediately.

Per serving: calories, 440; CHO, 56 g; PRO, 19 g; fat, 18 g; water, 78%

Characteristics: high calorie and protein, good amount of calcium. Quick to prepare, this is a meal in a glass.

Special Rice
(HOT)
MAKES 4 (¾-CUP) SERVINGS

This is a great way to reintroduce milk into the diet after a bout of sickness. It's also good for people who hate milk or who are marginally lactose-intolerant.

Sometimes milk can taste or smell to a pregnant woman like the cardboard carton it comes in. The solution: buy milk in glass or plastic bottles. Don't store milk next to the onions in the refrigerator, either.

For a change of pace, try fragrant Basmati rice or add 1 or 2 drops of vanilla or lemon extract during the final phase of cooking.

Cook 1 cup of rice slowly in 2½ to 3 cups of low-fat milk until the rice is soft. Stir often and add small amounts of water if the milk is absorbed before the rice is tender. Serve hot or cold. Or add extra hot milk and cinnamon and eat like a porridge any time of the day.

Per serving: calories, 260; CHO, 45 g; PRO, 9 g; fat, 4 g; water, 73%

Characteristics: high calcium, bland, can be eaten hot *or* cold

Tangy Pear Salad

(PUNGENT)

MAKES 4 SERVINGS

2 fresh pears, thinly sliced (leave the peel on)
1 cup seedless red or green grapes
3 tbsp coarsely chopped walnuts
2 tbsp honey or Lyle's Golden Syrup
2 tbsp fresh lime juice
1 tbsp vegetable oil
1 t poppy seeds (or sesame seeds)
⅛ t salt
⅛ t ground allspice

1. Combine pears, grapes, and walnuts.
2. Toss with remaining ingredients.
3. Serve on romaine lettuce. Add ½ cup cottage cheese to each serving if desired.

Per serving (with cottage cheese): calories, 207; CHO, 31 g; PRO, 6 g; fat, 8 g; water, 73%

Per serving (without cottage cheese): calories, 181; CHO, 30 g; PRO, 2 g; fat, 8 g; water, 73%

Characteristics: high natural water content, high calcium, vitamins, lots of fiber and texture, colorful; tanginess can be controlled

Cranberry Pudding
(SWEET)

MAKES 6 (2/3-CUP) SERVINGS

4 cups cranberry juice
½ cup sugar or honey to taste if using unsweetened juice
¼ cup potato starch
⅓ cup cold water

1. Put juice (and sugar if used) into saucepan and heat, but do not boil.
2. Mix potato starch slowly with cold water to make paste and pour slowly into juice. Stir well with wire whisk.
3. Simmer pudding until thickened and translucent.
4. Remove from heat. Sprinkle with sugar if desired and serve chilled. Add whipped cream or yogurt if you wish.

Per serving: calories, 110; CHO, 27 g; PRO, 1 g; fat, 1 g; water, 83%

Characteristics: sweet and tart, thick liquid, easily digested carbohydrates

Lemon Soup
(SOUR)

MAKES 6 (2/3-CUP) SERVINGS

4 cups water
¼ cup raisins
¼ cup sugar (to taste)
1 cinnamon stick
3 tbsp barley flour or potato starch
⅓ cup cold water
juice of 1 or 2 lemons, or more if desired

1. Put water, raisins, sugar, and cinnamon in saucepan and bring to a boil. Cover and simmer 10 minutes, then remove from heat.
2. Mix flour or starch slowly with cold water, making smooth paste, and add slowly to above mixture, stirring with whisk.
3. Reheat about 10 minutes and discard cinnamon stick.
4. When soup has thickened, remove from heat and stir in lemon juice. Serve chilled, with or without sugar sprinkled on top, or with whipped cream or yogurt.

Per serving: calories, 80; CHO, 20 g; PRO, 1 g; fat, 1 g; water, 90%

Characteristics: tangy, smooth, thick liquid, easily digested carbohydrate

Homemade Ginger Ale

(SPICY)

MAKES 4 (10-OZ) SERVINGS

This recipe is another used with the permission of Nancy Clark, R.D., M.S., author of *Nancy Clark's Sports Nutrition Cookbook.* Nancy Clark, incidentally, was affected by nausea in both of her pregnancies, and has written about her experiences in an article "When Eating for Two Wasn't Easy." Nancy's books contain other great quick recipes for healthful eating.

In the Orient, ginger has been touted for years as a natural antinauseant, which may explain why some women with nausea gravitate to the more tart and tangy ginger ales. But authorities are quick to point out that there is a difference between fresh and dried gingers, and between ginger from the West and that from the Orient. If you find ginger helpful, try ginger conserves on your morning toast.

2 tbsp fresh ginger root, chopped
rinds of 2 lemons
3–4 tbsp honey or other sweetner to taste
1 cup boiling water
1 quart seltzer (cold)

1. Put ginger and lemon rinds in a small bowl with honey.
2. Pour in 1 cup boiling water (or just enough to cover). Let steep for 5 minutes.
3. Strain and chill.
4. When ready to serve, add chilled seltzer.

Spicy Fruit Soup

(SPICY)

MAKES 6 (8-OZ) SERVINGS

2 medium oranges, peeled and cut into sections
1 medium peach, or 2 canned peach halves in light juice
1 large nectarine
½ cup lemon juice
1 tbsp orange juice concentrate
5 tbsp sugar
2 t cornstarch
3 cups orange juice
pinch of salt
2 sticks of cinnamon
¼ t ground cloves
2 tbsp flour
Optional: thinly sliced orange for garnish

1. Place chopped orange sections in bowl. In another bowl, mix chopped peach and nectarine. Toss with 2 t of the lemon juice. Set aside.
2. In a large saucepan, combine sugar and cornstarch. Gradually add orange and remaining lemon juice, salt, and spices.
3. Bring liquid to a boil over high heat, stirring for about 1 minute. Reduce heat and continue to simmer for 5 to 10 minutes.
4. Add chopped peach and nectarine to liquid and simmer again for 5 minutes. Remove pan from heat and allow to cool about 30 minutes. Add reserved chopped orange sections. Refrigerate several hours or overnight before serving. Garnish with orange slices if desired.

Per serving: calories, 155; CHO, 38 g; PRO, 2 g; fat, 1 g; water, 82%

Characteristics: tangy, high water content, high fiber

Extraordinary Noodles
(TANGY)

MAKES 4 LARGE SERVINGS

12 oz of pasta noodles (vary the shape for interest)
1½ tbsp poppy seeds
¼ cup soft-spread corn-oil margarine
½ t ground nutmeg
1 t freshly grated lemon rind
½ t salt
pepper to taste

1. Cook pasta in salted water as directed on package. Drain and keep hot.
2. Toast the poppy seeds by placing them in an ungreased sauté pan over medium heat. Stir or shake often for 5 to 10 minutes. Let cool for 1 or 2 minutes.
3. Blend margarine, nutmeg, lemon rind, and toasted poppyseeds in small bowl.
4. Toss all ingredients in warmed serving dish and serve immediately.

Per serving: calories, 220; CHO, 22 g; PRO, 4 g; fat, 13 g; water, 60%

Characteristics: spicy and bland together, reheats well

Quick Fruit Salad
(TANGY)

MAKES 4 (½-CUP) SERVINGS

1 peeled and sliced kiwi fruit
1 cup hulled fresh strawberries
1 cup grapes, black or green (or mixed)
8 oz plain yogurt
¼ cup freshly squeezed lemon
1–2 t freshly grated lemon peel

1. Mix all fruit together.
2. Mix yogurt and lemon juice and peel.
3. Toss fruit with yogurt. Refrigerate any unused portion. (Or blend yogurt and kiwi in blender, add rest of fruit, and freeze in popsicle molds.)

Per serving: calories, 90; CHO, 13 g; PRO, 4 g; fat, 1 g; water, 85%

Characteristics: tangy, high fiber, high potassium, high vitamin C

Lime Pudding

(TANGY)

MAKES 4 (1/2-CUP) SERVINGS

For a change, use lemon instead of lime.

2 tbsp sugar
1½ tbsp cornstarch mixed with equal amount cold water
1 t margarine
¼ cup lime juice
4 oz evaporated skim milk
4 oz plain yogurt
1½ t freshly grated lime rind

1. In saucepan over medium heat, mix first 5 ingredients. Cook slowly, stirring frequently, until thickened.
2. Remove from stove and pour into chilled "oven-to-freezer" baking dish. When cooled, stir in last 2 ingredients.
3. Serve immediately.

Per serving: calories, 85; CHO, 15 g; PRO, 4 g; fat, 2 g; water, 73%

Characteristics: tart, smooth, high nutritional value, high calcium source

Refreshing Asparagus
(TANGY)

MAKES 4 (3-STALK) SERVINGS

1 bunch fresh young light-green asparagus
2 tbsp corn-oil margarine
3 tbsp lemon juice
1 orange juice concentrate

1. Trim woody ends off asparagus. Place in 9-inch pie plate with 1 tbsp water and cover tightly with plastic wrap. Microwave on high for 45 seconds or until crisp-tender. Poke with fork to check tenderness. Remicrowave if necessary. Drain.
2. Melt margarine in glass measuring cup in microwave on low.
3. Add 2 juices and stir.
4. Pour sauce over hot asparagus and serve immediately.

Per serving: calories, 82; CHO, 5 g; PRO, 2 g; fat, 6 g; water, 90%

Characteristics: quick cooking, high fiber, good source of potassium: can be eaten cold

Indian Yogurt Drink (Lassi)

(WET)

MAKES 4 (1-CUP) SERVINGS

You can make a large portion of this and freeze it.

8 oz plain yogurt
2 pints water
ice cubes
1 t dried mint
1 t salt

1. Mix yogurt and water in large pitcher.
2. Add mint and salt and mix well.
3. Add ice cubes and serve.

Per serving: calories, 36; CHO, 4 g; PRO, 3 g; fat, 1 g; water, 94%

Characteristics: cool, refreshing aroma, good way to work in dairy products after a hiatus, thirst-quenching

Grapefruit-Cucumber Salad

(TART)

MAKES 4 SERVINGS

1 large cucumber, sliced thin (about 1 cup)
2 peeled large grapefruit or 3 cups grapefruit sections
2 tbsp vegetable oil
2 tbsp cider vinegar
2 tbsp sugar (or to taste)
¼ t dill

Toss all ingredients together in large bowl. Serve on chilled plates.

Per serving: calories, 134; CHO, 19 g; PRO, 2 g; fat, 7 g; water, 87%

Characteristics: high fiber, high water content

Buttermilk-Fruit Soup

(TANGY)

MAKES 4 SERVINGS

1¼ cup cleaned fresh berries (blueberries, blackberries or strawberries)
1 large banana
2 cups skim milk buttermilk
⅓ cup sugar
juice and grated lemon rind (from ½ lemon)
1 t almond or vanilla extract

1. Place berries, buttermilk and sugar in blender and blend for 30 seconds.
2. Pour into large bowl and stir in lemon rind, lemon juice and extract flavor of your choice.
3. Chill. Pour into serving bowls and garnish with berries or freshly washed mint leaves.

Per serving: calories, 170; CHO, 36 g; PRO, 5 g; fat, 2 g

Characteristics: high potassium, good calcium source, very low fat (cultured buttermilk is especially good for lactose-intolerant persons)

Avocado Whip
(EARTHY)
MAKES 4 SERVINGS

1 avocado, peeled and pitted
juice of one lemon
2 tbsp sugar
1 cup vanilla ice milk

1. Mash avocado and put through sieve.
2. Add lemon juice and sugar.
3. Add ice milk and whip with beater until smooth
4. Place in freezer to chill, but do not freeze.

Per serving: calories, 100; CHO, 12 g; PRO, 2 g; fat, 6 g

Characteristics: earthy and smooth, good potassium source

Maple Tofu Ice Cream
(SWEET)
MAKES 8 SERVINGS

14 ounces soft tofu
1¼ cups evaporated milk (or heavy cream if you prefer)
⅔ cup maple syrup.

1. Blend all ingredients in blender.
2. Place blender container in freeze and chill until almost frozen.
3. Puree again.
4. Pour into separate dessert cups.
5. Optional topping: Mix ⅓ cup each chopped almonds, chopped figs, shredded coconut with 2 tbsp brown sugar.

Per serving (without topping): calories, 135; CHO, 22 g; PRO, 7 g; fat, 2 g

Characteristics: earthy and smooth, good source of calcium, protein, iron, potassium

"Easy Refrigerator" Pie

(EARTHY)

MAKES 8 SERVINGS

2 tbsp cold water
1 envelope plain gelatin
1 cup boiling water
8 ounces "light" or low-fat cream cheese (or half soft tofu and
   half low-fat cream cheese)
¼ cup sugar
1 cup vanilla ice milk
8–9 inch graham cracker crust or gingersnap cookie crust
Optional: pinch of butter-flavored salt and bottled lemon peel.

1. Put cold water and gelatin into blender and allow to sit for
   about 1 minute.
2. Add hot water and blend on high for two minutes or until
   gelatin dissolved.
3. Add cream cheese, sugar, flavorings and blend again.
4. Add ice milk and blend again. Put covered container into
   the refrigerator for 15–20 minutes until thickened.
5. Pour into crust and chill for about 2 hours. Top with
   freshly sliced peaches tossed with lemon juice. Sprinkle
   with small amount of granulated sugar.

Per serving: calories, 350; CHO, 42 g; PRO, 6 g; fat, 18 g

Per serving (½-tofu version): calories, 323; CHO, 42 g; PRO, 6 g; fat, 16 g

Characteristics: smooth and earthy, good source potassium

Lemon Brown Rice and Chicken Casserole
(EARTHY/TART)

MAKE 4 SERVINGS

1 tbsp olive oil
½ cup finely chopped onion (about 1 small)
1 garlic clove minced
1 cup raw brown rice
2¼ cup fresh chicken broth
¼ cup freshly squeezed lemon juice (or orange juice)
2 t grated lemon rind (or orange peel)
4 ounces chicken breast, cut into ¼" × 2" strips.
seasonings to taste

1. Sauté onion and garlic in olive oil over medium heat.
2. Add rice and chicken pieces and stir to cover. Add broth, juice, rind, and salt and pepper if you choose.
3. Bring to a boil, cover and reduce heat. Allow to simmer for 45 minutes or until liquid has been absorbed and rice is done and fluffy.
4. Garnish with freshly chopped parsley or sauteed almond slivers if you choose.

Per serving: calories, 280, CHO, 40 g; PRO, 15 g; FAT, 7 g

Characteristics: earthy and tart, good fiber source, low fat, variable; pack in microwavable container to heat at work for lunch

Cherry Mousse

(TART/COLD)

MAKES 6 SERVINGS

2 cups canned drained sour cherries (or any canned fruit, drained)
1 cup plain yogurt
⅓ cup brown sugar
1½ t almond extract
4 egg whites

1. Blend cherries with yogurt, sugar, extract.
2. In a separate bowl, beat egg whites until stiff peaks form.
3. Pour the cherry mixture into large mixing bowl and fold in egg whites.
4. Pour into serving dishes and freeze. Allow 10 minutes to unfreeze before eating.

Per serving: calories, 110; CHO, 22 g; PRO, 5 g; fat, 1 g

Characteristics: cold, tart, smooth, good way to work dairy products back into diet

A P P E N D I X

Recommended Dietary Allowances (underweight)

Name: Mrs. Mom (underweight); Age, 30; Sex, F; Pregnant Weight, 110 lb; Height, 5 ft, 5 in; Sedentary

Calories	1942 *	Pyridoxine—B6	2.20 mg
Protein	50.0 g	Cobalamin—B12	2.20 mcg
Carbohydrates	238 g **	Folacin	400 mcg
Dietary fiber	16.4 g #	Pantothenic	7.00 mg *
Fat—total	54.7 g **	Vitamin C	70.0 mg
Fat—saturated	18.2 g **	Vitamin E	10.0 mg
Fat—mono	18.2 g **	Calcium	1200 mg
Fat—poly	18.2 g **	Copper	2.50 mg *
Cholesterol	300 mg **	Iron	30.0 mg
Vitamin A—carotene	RE	Magnesium	320 mg
Vitamin A—preformed	RE	Phosphorus	1200 mg
Vitamin A—total	800 RE	Potassium	2000 mg *
Thiamin—B1	1.40 mg	Selenium	65.0 mcg
Riboflavin—B2	1.50 mg	Sodium	2400 mg *
Niacin—B3	15.0 mg	Zinc	15.0 mg

* Suggested values; within recommended ranges.
** Dietary goals.
# Fiber = 1 g/100 kcal.

Recommended Dietary Allowances (Average Weight)

Name: Mrs. Mom (average weight); Age, 30; Sex, F; Pregnant Weight,
130 lb; Height, 5 ft, 5 in; Sedentary

Calories	2052 *	Pyridoxine—B6	2.20 mg
Protein	57.3 g	Cobalamin—B12	2.20 mcg
Carbohydrates	254 g **	Folacin	400 mcg
Dietary fiber	17.5 g #	Pantothenic	7.00 mg *
Fat—total	58.4 g **	Vitamin C	70.0 mg
Fat—saturated	19.5 g **	Vitamin E	10.0 mg
Fat—mono	19.5 g **	Calcium	1200 mg
Fat—poly	19.5 g **	Copper	2.50 mg *
Cholesterol	300 mg **	Iron	30.0 mg
Vitamin A—carotene	RE	Magnesium	320 mg
Vitamin A—preformed	RE	Phosphorus	1200 mg
Vitamin A—total	800 RE	Potassium	2000 mg *
Thiamin—B1	1.40 mg	Selenium	65.0 mcg
Riboflavin—B2	1.50 mg	Sodium	2400 mg *
Niacin—B3	15.0 mg	Zinc	15.0 mg

* Suggested values; within recommended ranges.
** Dietary goals.
# Fiber = 1 g/100 kcal.

Recommended Dietary Allowances (Overweight)

Name: Mrs. Mom (overweight); Age, 30; Sex, F; Pregnant Weight, 180 lb;
Height, 5 ft, 5 in; Sedentary

Calories	2327 *	Pyridoxine—B6	2.20 mg
Protein	75.5 g	Cobalamin—B12	2.20 mcg
Carbohydrates	294 g **	Folacin	400 mcg
Dietary fiber	20.3 g #	Pantothenic	7.00 mg *
Fat—total	67.6 g **	Vitamin C	70.0 mg
Fat—saturated	22.5 g **	Vitamin E	10.0 mg
Fat—mono	22.5 g **	Calcium	1200 mg
Fat—poly	22.5 g **	Copper	2.50 mg *
Cholesterol	300 mg **	Iron	30.0 mg
Vitamin A—Carotene	RE	Magnesium	320 mg
Vitamin A—Preformed	RE	Phosphorus	1200 mg
Vitamin A—Total	800 RE	Potassium	2000 mg *
Thiamin—B1	1.41 mg	Selenium	65.0 mcg
Riboflavin—B2	1.52 mg	Sodium	2400 mg *
Niacin—B3	15.4 mg	Zinc	15.0 mg

* Suggested values; within recommended ranges.
** Dietary goals.
# Fiber = 1 g/100 kcal.

THE TONGUE

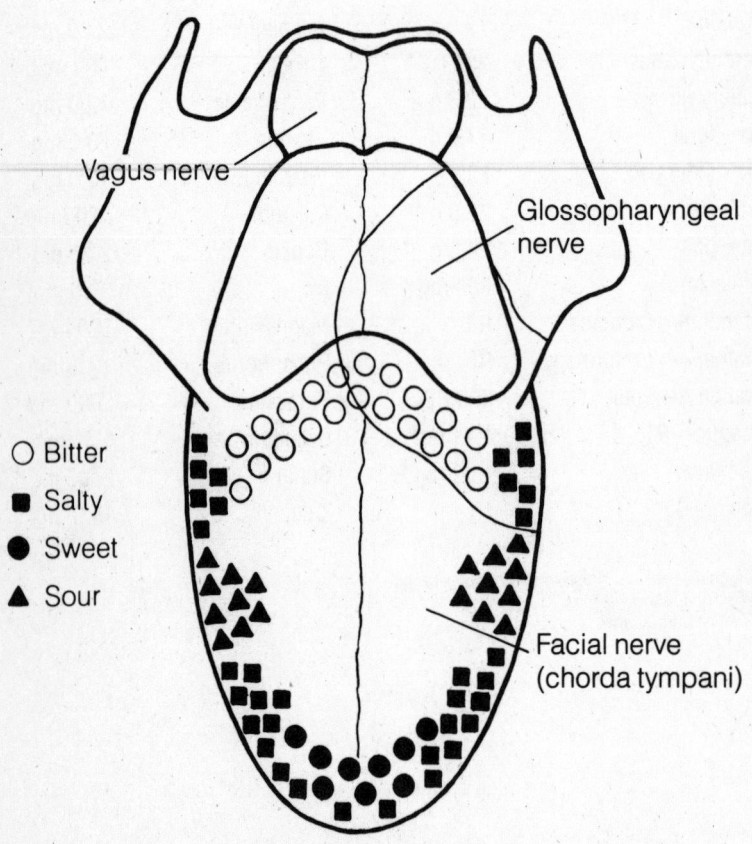

How to use the Weight Change Chart

If you were underweight before you became pregnant, you're expected to gain more weight. If you were within your desirable body weight limits, as defined by the 1959 Metropolitan Weight Tables, your weight gain in pregnancy can be less than that of an underweight woman. Being overweight before pregnancy means your weight gain can be slightly below these previous recommendations. Refer to the chart with the weight gain curves. The "twin pregnancy" weight curve is the first; underweight is next, followed by overweight and obese.

Although the 1983 Metropolitan Life Insurance Weight Charts have been issued and allow people to weigh a bit more and still be considered "within normal limits," some clinicians believe that using the 1959 charts is preferable, as they're the weight parameters used currently by the National Education and Cholesterol Program. The 1959 standards are the ones I currently use.

Please note that weight gain is not the only criterion for a successful and healthy pregnancy. Women who have problems in pregnancy, notably diabetes and high blood pressure, or those who foolishly continue to smoke, may gain "according to recommendations" yet have small babies. Monitoring weight is *only* one part of your medical care. A weight loss in pregnancy does not mean your baby will have severe problems, either, although it's to be avoided if possible. Being in good shape nutritionally before becoming pregnant is the smartest thing you can do for yourself.

Daily Fluid Needs

Your body requires a certain amount of fluid each and every day to maintain good health. The exact amount varies depending on a person's size, climatic conditions, level of exercise and physical activity. People living at high altitudes and in hot places need more fluid. This guide has been created for a sea-level, average temperature environment for the average 5' 5", 125 pound woman. Ask your doctor if you require additional fluids.

Adequate hydration is one of the main factors to prevent dehy-

WEIGHT CHANGE CHART

date of last menstrual cycle:＿＿＿＿＿＿
prepregnancy weight:＿＿＿＿＿＿ date:＿＿＿＿＿＿
due date:＿＿＿＿＿ (dated by your M.D.)
Begin dating this chart by the dates your doctor gives you. This may be two weeks
different from your particular dates. Doctors have been dating from a lunar calendar
for centuries, and this is not about to change soon! You can make another copy of this
chart if you wish, to use according to *your* method before your first prenatal visit.

Week No.	Date	New Weight	Change from Last Week	Comments
1				
2				
3				
4				
5				
6				
7				
8				
9				
10				
11				
12				
13				
14				
15				
16				
17				
18				
19				
20				
21				
22				
23				
24				
25				
26				
27				
28				
29				
30				
31				
32				
33				
34				
35				
36				
37				
38				
39				
40				
41				
42	(overdue!)			

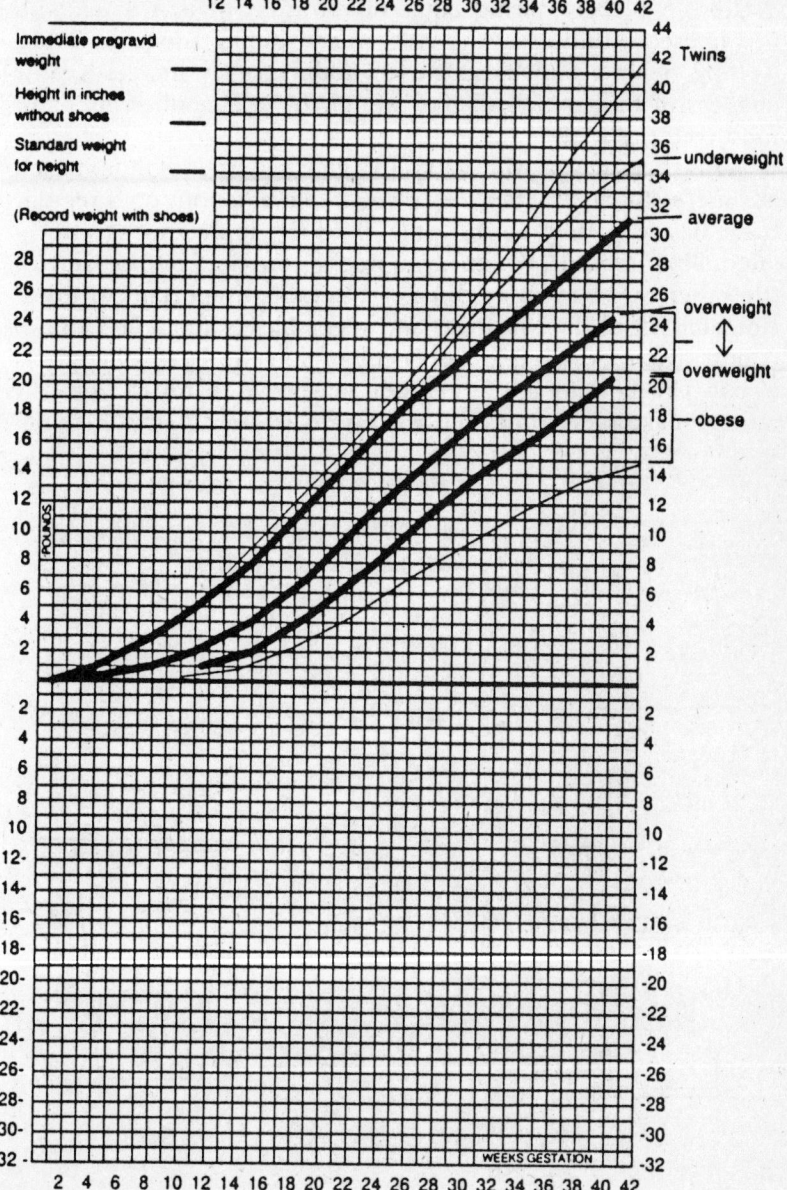

Pattern of normal prenatal gain in weight.
Source: Adapted from U.S. Department of health Education and Welfare, Social and Rehabilitation Service, Children's Bureau.

dration, especially during bouts of vomiting. Many women who feel nauseous find great difficulty in consuming adequate fluids. Getting behind the "fluid curve" today greatly increases your chances of having a "bad day" tomorrow. Remember, fluids in food count as well!

This chart may provide you with a gauge to types of fluids which are successful at certain times if you make notations on a regular basis. Besides jotting down type of fluid (ie, apple juice vs. chocolate milk), amount (¼ cup), you might note time of day some of the other variables we've discussed as being important to track. The amount of fluid in fruits and vegetables is about 50-75%, so count 1 cup of watermelon as ¾ cup of water and a small apple as ¼ cup. Crackers are low fluid foods, maybe 1 tbsp. for 10. You may want to make a few copies of this diagram before you start tracking.

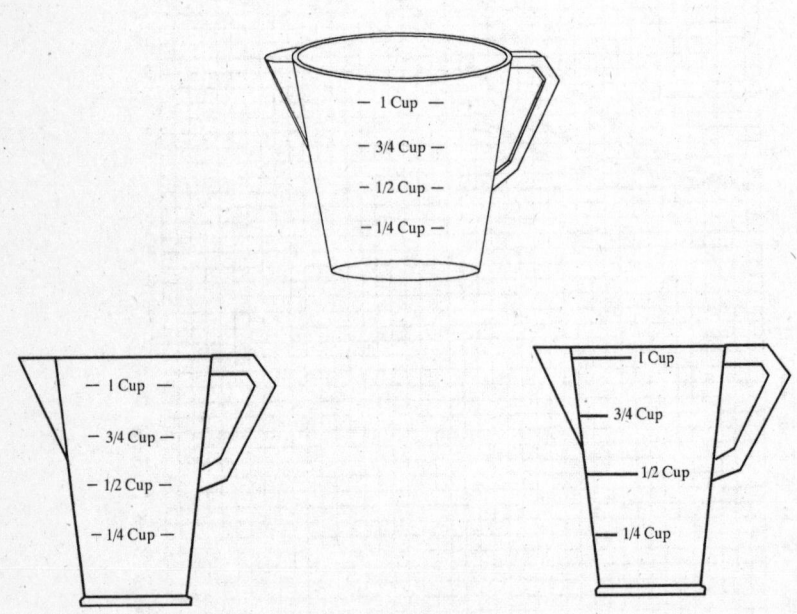

SELECTED REFERENCES

Introduction

Kemp, W. N. Hyperemesis gravidarum treated as a temporary adrenal cortex insufficiency. *The Lancet* (April 1933): 389–91.

Chapter 1: What Is Morning Sickness, Anyway?

FitzGerald, C. M. Nausea and vomiting in pregnancy. *British Journal of Medical Psychology, 57* (1984): 159–65

Vellacott, I. D., et al. Nausea and vomiting in early pregnancy. *International Journal of Gynecology and Obstetrics, 27* (1988): 57–62.

Jarnsfelt-Samsoie, A., et al. Nausea and vomiting in pregnancy—a contribution to its epidemiology. *Gynecology and Obstetrics Investigation, 16* (1983): 221–29

Getchell, Doty, & Bartoshuk, Snow (Eds.). *Smell and taste in health and disease.* New York: Raven Press, 1991.

Tierson, F. D., et al. Nausea and vomiting of pregnancy and association with pregnancy outcome. *American Journal of Obstetrics and Gynecology, 155* (1986): 1017–22.

Walters, W. A. W. The management of nausea and vomiting of pregnancy. *Medical Journal of Australia, 147* (Sept. 21, 1987): 290–91.

DiLorio, C. The management of nausea and vomiting of pregnancy. *Nurse Practitioner* (May 1988): 23–28.

Koch, K. L. Gastric dysrhythmias and nausea of pregnancy. *Digestive Diseases Science, 35*, 8 (Aug. 1990) 961–68.

Worthington-Roberts, B., & Williams, S. R. Physiology of pregnancy. In *Nutrition in pregnancy and lactation* (4th ed.). St. Louis, MO: Times Mirror/Mosby, 1989, 23–46.

Minturn, L., & Wylie Weiher, A. Influence of diet on morning sickness: a cross cultural study. *Medical Anthropology* (Winter 1984): 71–75.

Profet, M. The function of allergy: immunological defense against toxins. *Quarterly Review of Biology, 66*, 1 (March 1991): 23–66.

Samsioe, G. Does position and size of the corpus luteum have any effect on nausea of pregnancy? *Acta Obstetrics and Gynecology, 65* (1986): 427.

Chapter 2: If You're Miserable, You're in Good Company

Bolte, P. The treatment of pregnancy nausea. Simmons College (Boston, MA) Graduate Program in Primary Health Care Nursing. Master of Science Nursing Thesis, 1989.

Zubek, L., et al. Significance of blood flow measurement in the cervix uteri in the first trimester of pregnancy. *Zentralbi Gynakol, 108*, 15 (1986): 900–905 (in German).

David, M. First trimester pregnancy. *American Journal of Nursing* (Dec. 1976): 1945–48.

Feingold, M. K., et al. Bulimia nervosa in pregnancy: a case report. *Obstetrics and Gynecology, 71*, 6, part 2 (June 1988): 1025–27.

Chapter 3: A Candid Look at Feelings

Tanner, I. J. *The gift of grief.* New York: Hawthorn, 1976.

Tarvis, C. *Anger: The misunderstood emotion.* New York: Touchstone/Simon and Schuster, 1982.

Chapter 4: The Role of Nutrition

Krzywicki, H. J., et al. Metabolic aspects of acute starvation. *American Journal of Clinical Nutrition, 21,* 1 (Jan. 1968): 87–97.

Tegner, B. *The survival book.* New York: Bantam, 1983.

Angier, B. *Survival with style.* New York: National Wildlife Federation/Vintage, 1972.

Fiorucci, et al. Duodenal osmolality drives gallbladder emptying in humans. *Digestive Diseases Sciences, 35,* 6 (Aug./Sept. 1990).

Klawansky, S., & Chalmers, T. C. Fat content of very low calorie diets and gallstone formation (letter). *Journal of the American Medical Association* (Aug. 19, 1992): 873.

Chapter 5: Managing Morning Sickness with Food

Ayensu, E. S. *Medicinal plants of West Africa.* Algonac, MI: Reference Publications, 1978.

Medicinal plants in China (Compiled by the Institute of Chinese Materia Medica). WHO Regional Publications. Western Pacific Series No. 2. China Academy of Traditional Chinese Medicine, 1989.

Der Marderosian, A., & Liberti, L. *Natural product medicine: A scientific guide to foods, drugs, cosmetics.* Philadelphia: Stickney, 1988.

Chakraberty, C. *A comparative Hindu materia medica* (1923). Dehli: Neeraj, 1983.

Karasawa, K., and Shizuko, M. Taste preference and aversion in pregnancy. *Japanese Journal of Nutrition, 36,* 1: 31–37.

Harries, J. M., et al. An enumeration of the cravings of some pregnant women. *Proceedings of the Nutrition Society* (London), *16* (1957): xx–xxi.

Taggart, N. Food habits in pregnancy. *Proceedings of the Nutrition Society* (London), *20* (1961): 35–40.

Fisher-Rasmussen, W., et al. Ginger treatment of hyperemesis gravidarum. *European Journal of Obstetrics and Gynecological Reproductive Biology, 38* (1990): 19–24.

Barton, D., and Ollis, W. D. *Advances in medicinal phytochemistry.* Centre de Recherche Pierre Fabre. John Libbey, 1986.

Saunders, F., et al. Adsorption of physiologically substances by activated charcoal. *Proceedings of the Society of Experimental Biology, 28.* New York: W.B. Saunders, 1930–31, 564.

Gorman, W. *Flavor, taste and the psychology of smell.* Springfield, IL: Charles Thomas, 1964.

Chapter 6: Noses: Regular and Premium

World Resources Institute. How perfumes pollute. In *The 1993 Information Please Environmental Almanac.* Boston, MA: Houghton Mifflin, 1993, 92.

Gandelman, R. Gonadal hormones and sensory function. *Neuroscience and Biobehavioral Reviews, 7* (1983): 1–17.

Winter, R. *The smell book.* Philadelphia: J.B. Lippincott, 1976.

Apfel, R. J., et al. The role of hypnotizability in the pathogenesis and treatment of nausea and vomiting of pregnancy. *Journal of Psychosomatic Obstetrics and Gynecology, 5* (1986): 179–86.

Yerushalmy, J. & Milkovich, L. Evaluation of teratogenic effect of meclizine in man. *American Journal of Obstetrics and Gynecology* (Oct. 15, 1965): 553–62.

Davis, C. J., Lake-Bakaar, G. V., and Grahame-Smith, D. G. *Nausea and vomiting* (Berlin/New York: Springer-Verlag, n.d.).

Chapter 7: Other Times and Other Places

Dobelis, I. N. (Project Ed.). *Magic and medicine of plants.* Pleasantville, NY: Reader's Digest, 1986.

Gaskell, E. *The life of Charlotte Brontë* (1857). New York: E.P. Dutton, 1971.

Vermeer, D. Geophagy among the Tiv of Nigeria. *Annuals of the Association of American Geographers, 56,* 2 (June 1966): 197–204.

———. Geophagy among the Eve of Ghana. *Ethnology, 10* (1971): 56–72.

Richardson, M. & Davidson, W. Earth as the Lord's Bread: the cultural world of geophagy in Esquilpulas, Guatamala (manuscript in preparation). Department of Geography and Anthropology, Louisiana State University, Baton Rouge, LA (personal communication Oct. 18, 1991).

Kay, M. A. Health and illness in a Mexican American barrio. In Spice, E. W. (Ed.), *Ethnic medicine in the southwest,* Tucson: University of Arizona Press, 1977.

Solo, S. Scents to make you work harder. *Fortune* (Feb. 27, 1989): 8.

Bricklin, M. *The practical encyclopedia of natural healing.* Rodale, 1976, 462.

Chapter 8: Morning Sickness Is Not in the Head

Tylden, E. Hyperemesis and physiological vomiting. *Journal of Psychosomatic Research, 12* (1968): 85–93.

Fairweather, D. V. I. Nausea and vomiting in pregnancy. *American Journal of Obstetrics and Gynecology* (Sept. 1, 1968): 135–75.

Robertson, G. G. Nausea and vomiting of pregnancy: A study in psychosomatic and social medicine. *The Lancet* (Sept. 7, 1946): 336–41.

Hill, O. W. Psychogenic vomiting. *Gut, 9* (1968): 348–52.

Macy, C. Psychological factors in nausea and vomiting of pregnancy: A review. *Journal of Reproductive and Infant Psychology, 4* (1986): 23–55.

Sahakian, V., et al. Vitamin B6 is effective therapy for nausea and vomiting of pregnancy: A randomized, double blind, placebo-controlled trial. *Obstetrics and Gynecology, 78* (1991): 33–36.

Erick, M., to Sahakian, V. (personal communication), Nov. 14, 1991.

Sahakian, V. (personal communication), Dec. 17, 1991.

Schuster, K., et al. Morning sickness and vitamin B6 status of pregnant women. *Human Nutrition: Clinical Nutrition* (1985): 39C, 75–79.

De Aloysio, D., & Penacchioni, P. Morning sickness control in early pregnancy by Neiguan point accupressure. *Obstetrics and Gynecology, 80* (1992): 852–54.

Finger, T., & Silver, W. *Neurobiology of taste and smell.* New York: Wiley, 1987.

Doty, R., et al. Smell identification ability: Changes with age. *Science, 226* (1986): 1441–43.

————. Endocrine, cardiovascular and psychological correlates of olfactory sensitivity and changes during the menstrual cycle. *Journal of Comparative Physiology, 95,* 1 (1981): 45–60.

Chapter 9: Special Concerns

LeGoff D., et al. Salivary response to olfactory food stimuli in anorexics and bulimics. *Appetite, 11* (1988): 15–22.

Suddick, R. Salivary Na^+, K^+ and Cl^- secretion rates: Relationship to a fluid generation mechanism. *Japanese Journal of Physiology, 20* (1970): 540–49.

Barton, J. R., at al. Baking powder pica mimicking preeclampsia. *American Journal of Obstetrics and Gynecology, 167* (1992): 98–99.

Horner, R. D., at al. Pica practices of pregnant women. *Journal of the American Dietetic Association, 91* (1991): 34–38.

Chapter 10: Worst-Case Scenario: Being Hospitalized

Commission on Professional and Hospital Activities. LOS: Length of stay. Length of stay by diagnosis. Northeastern Region, 1985. Ann Arbor, MI: CPHA Publications, October 1986, 4, 150.

Chapter 11: Your Survival Kit

Olkin, S. K. *Positive pregnancy fitness.* Garden City Park, NJ: Avery, 1987.

Ackerman, D. *A natural history of the senses.* New York: Random House, 1991.

Walker, A. R. P., et al. Nausea and vomiting and dietary cravings and aversions during pregnancy in South African women. *British Journal of Obstetrics and Gynecology, 92* (May 1985): 484–89.

Hunter, J. M., et al. Religious geophagy as a cottage industry: The holy clay tablet of Esquipulas, Guatemala. *National Geographic Research, 5,* 3 (1989): 281–95.

Chapter 12: The Importance of D.I.E.T.

Erick, M. *D.I.E.T. during pregnancy: The complete guide and calendar.* Brookline, MA: Grinnen-Barrett, 1987.

Smith, P., & Coats, C. *Perfectly pregnant.* Orlando, FL: Carolyn Coats Bestsellers, 1988.

Swinney, B. *Eating expectly.* Colorado Springs: CO. Fall River, 1993.

Chapter 15: Recipes and Menus

Clark, N. *Nancy Clark's sports nutrition guidebook.* Champaign, IL: Leisure Press, 1990.

Haroutunian, A. *A Turkish cookbook.* London: Ebury Press, 1987.

Ortiz, E. L. *The complete book of Caribbean cooking.* New York: Ballantine, 1973.

Merchant, I. *Ismail Merchant's Indian cuisine.* New York: Fireside/Simon and Schuster, 1986.

Hachfeld, L., & Eykyn, B. *Cooking à la heart.* Mankato, MN: Apple Tree Press, 1992.

Kakonen, U. *Natural cooking the Finnish way.* New York: Quadrangle, 1974.

Index

 **PLUME**

HELPFUL ADVICE

 **PLUME**

PREGNANCY, BIRTH, AND CHILDCARE